A BIRD LOVER'S LIFE LIST & JOURNAL

Mountain Bluebird, Townsend's Warbler, & Western Bluebird
(Arctic Blue-bird, Townsend's Warbler & Western Blue-bird, PLATE CCCXCIII)

edited and with an introduction by NORMAN BOUCHER

with illustrations by JOHN JAMES AUDUBON

A BIRD LOVER'S LIFE LIST & JOURNAL

A BULFINCH PRESS BOOK

LITTLE, BROWN AND COMPANY

BOSTON · TORONTO · LONDON

First Edition

Quote on page ix from *Audubon: A Vision* © Estate of Robert Penn Warren, 1969. Published by Random House, 1969.

Quotes in marginalia are from the writings of John James Audubon.

Library of Congress Cataloging-in-Publication Data
A Bird lover's life list & journal / compiled and edited by Norman Boucher
     p.   cm.
Includes index.
ISBN 0-87846-356-9 (MFA)
ISBN 0-8212-1993-6 (BULFINCH)
 I. Bird watching. 2 Audubon. 3. Blank books.
 I. Boucher, Norman, 1951-
II. Title: Bird lover's life list & journal.

QL677.5.B4815 1992	92-9082
598'.07'2347 – dc20	CIP

Special thanks to Sue Reed and John Chvostal of the Prints and Drawing Department of the Museum of Fine Arts, Boston, and to Sheridan Behrmann, who helped make this publication possible.

Design by Christopher Frame
Project Coordinator: Kathryn Sky-Peck

Published by
MUSEUM OF FINE ARTS, BOSTON
and
BULFINCH PRESS
Bulfinch Press is an imprint and trademark of Little, Brown and Company (Inc.)
Published simultaneously in Canada by Little, Brown & Company (Canada) Limited

PRINTED AND BOUND IN HONG KONG

CONTENTS

LIST OF PLATES

The birds that appear in the plates in this volume are listed here by their modern names. Where plates appear in the book, Audubon's name for the bird, if it differs, has been added, as well as the original plate number of the work as it appeared in *The Birds of America*.

"Where can I go now, and visit nature undisturbed?"

—John James Audubon, *"The Labrador Journal,"* June 23, 1833

"We never know what we have lost, or what we have found.
We are only ourselves, and that promise.
Continue to walk in the world. Yes, love it!"

—Robert Penn Warren, *Audubon: A Vision*

Little Blue Heron (Blue Heron, PLATE CCCVII)

MOST BIRDERS I KNOW keep a Life List, a continuing record of species seen or heard. There are many ways of doing this, but most of us are content to use the lists provided in field guides. The procedure is simple. See a new lifer; put a checkmark beside its name. By writing in tiny letters, you might be able to squeeze in a date, too. But nothing more. The trouble with this system is that, over time, the list grows longer while memory grows shorter. The concrete details that evoke the cold salt wind of a sighting in Maine, the sweet primordial musk of a mangrove creek along the Gulf of Mexico, the ocher dust that settles on your shoes in an Arizona canyon – these blooms of experience are often buried under newer details of fresh sightings, like snow cloaking the wildflowers of fall.

Still, the penchant for listing that characterizes many birders doesn't stop at Life Lists. Some compulsives keep track of *everything*. For structure, they'll use any set of natural or manmade boundaries they can think of, listing, say, the birds they've seen within Everglades National Park, or inside the state of Texas, or within the property lines of their own backyards. There are even competitions to see who can compile the longest list within a given stretch of time, usually 24 hours, mad scrambles that must appear particularly odd from the birds' point of view. "A hurried man trying to identify a hurried bird," E.B. White once observed, "is palpably a ridiculous situation."

There exists, of course, no shortage of noble reasons for keeping lists. Doing so can be an aid to concentration, and concentration naturally deepens curiosity. Birders who look carefully see beyond plumage to behavior; they get an inkling of how little is really known about why birds do the endlessly absorbing things they do. Scratch a scientist or an environmentalist and you often find someone who as a child or an adolescent became enraptured by the outdoor kaleidoscope first mirrored in the glossy pages of Roger Tory Peterson's *A Field Guide to the Birds*. Look closely at the actual book and you will likely find checkmarks all over the section up front called "My Life List."

More importantly, good lists compiled by reliable field observers can help scientists track distribution and population trends; even casual birdwatchers can provide useful data to their local policymakers. A sudden drop in the number of American Redstart sightings on a five- or ten-year yard list, for example, can alert conservation commissioners that developers in town may have fragmented one woodland or filled in one wetland too many. In fact, now that the rapid and widespread loss of habitat has thrust record numbers of species toward the precipice of extinction, the habit of observing what birds are left out there is of greater importance

INTRO-DUCTION

than ever. At this moment more than 80 species and subspecies of birds are waiting to be evaluated for either endangered or threatened status under the federal Endangered Species Act; yet for at least a third of them so little is known about their numbers that any judgment on their fate can be little more than a guess.

But noble reasons for keeping bird lists often seem strained to me. After all, most of us never show our lists to anyone. We keep lists for the fun of it, as a way of stimulating a crowded memory into recall. Several weeks before writing this, for example, I saw my first Loggerhead Shrike (*Lanius ludovicianus*), one of those candidate species for the Endangered Species List that may or may not be disappearing. Like the similar Northern Shrike (*L. excubitor*), the Loggerhead is a songbird that thinks it's a hawk. It eats much the same food as a hawk – insects, lizards, mice, and small birds – but is built more delicately. Unable to hold onto its sometimes squirming meal, the shrike, ever resourceful, compensates by impaling its prey on a thorn or barb of fence wire before consuming it.

I was fortunate enough to see the Loggerhead do this. The sighting came at the end of a December week in and around the Florida Everglades. I was driving out of Everglades National Park en route to the Miami airport with a fellow birder. The week was done; one of our two pairs of binoculars was packed away. In the sawgrass prairies around us, thousands of spiderwebs were beaded with dew, an expanse of brocade momentarily illumined by the early morning sun. Suddenly from the driver's seat I spotted a gray bird perched in a small tree on the shoulder of the road. I made a U-turn and approached it slowly, using the car as a blind. I saw immediately that it was a shrike, but minutes passed before we could be certain it was a Loggerhead. As we watched, it darted suddenly to the ground, picked up a lizard with its hooked bill, and flew with it to another small tree in the sawgrass. With quick, sure movements it jammed the lizard in a fork among the branches and began to eat it. After five minutes of passing the binoculars back and forth, my friend and I remembered our own flight and drove away. The bird receded behind us and was lost in the infinite river of grass.

AUDUBON HIMSELF WOULD AGREE that such a sighting deserves more than a perfunctory checkmark on a crowded tally sheet. "I never for a day," he wrote, "gave up listening to the songs of our birds, or watching their peculiar habits, or delineating them in the best way that I could." Before his paintings, birds were commonly portrayed as stuffed specimens standing listless and erect. Audubon wired up freshly-killed birds and imagined them back into life. As Roger Tory Peterson has written, "He took birds out of the glass case for all time . . . ." His birds are usually in the middle of doing something; they exist in time as well as space.

Although Audubon died in 1851, long before people talked in terms of ecosystems and ecology, he envisioned birds in context, the context of a captured moment, full of the associations of nature and memory – he even sensed the beginning of their decline. Before binoculars, before cameras, before automobiles, Audubon vowed to paint a life-sized portrait of every species of American bird; his masterwork, *The Birds of America*, contains drawings of over 1,000 individuals. It is a determined, rhapsodic work, and whatever errors the ornithological nitpickers have found in it are errors of overexuberance. Nothing quite like it had ever been done before, or since.

This book, then, is for birders who believe in context and association, who wish for their Life Lists to capture birds in the middle of doing something. My recent shrike sighting, for instance, is precious to me not only because I'd never seen one before. I once had the opportunity to see one of the last Dusky Seaside Sparrows that ever lived, one of the last individuals of a now-extinct subspecies of Seaside Sparrows. The Dusky was living at the time in a small aviary in Gainesville, Florida, where it had been placed for its own protection. A technician brought me to the aviary and pointed out the bird, yet the memory remains shrouded in gray. It was the first Dusky I'd ever seen, and I knew it would be the last, yet the sighting seemed curiously joyless and abstracted. The DNA of the bird I saw certified that it was a Dusky, but removed forever from its free range, it already seemed less than a Dusky. Without its context, it was lost.

Given the dwindling numbers of Loggerhead Shrikes in the East, the one I saw in the Everglades may well be the last of its kind I'll ever see, too. But that experience contained all the surprise and texture that enliven a memorable sighting. The timing, the spiderwebs, the lizard – even the rental car – are details that made the bird an individual seen at a particular time and place and not merely a generalized representative of its species. These are details I want my Life List to make room for.

A Bird Lover's Life List & Journal is intended to provide that room. It is a place to record details about every species regularly found in North America, excluding Mexico. As such, it is meant to complement the birder's collection of field guides. It's a stay-at-home book, an album to rest on the lap after the day's birding is done. Over the years, I hope, it will contain a lifetime of birding memories, an anthology of first sightings vividly recorded. It is an ornithological biography in the making.

LIKE MOST RECENT FIELD GUIDES, the *Life List's* organization matches that of the sixth edition of the American Ornithologists' Union (A.O.U.) *Checklist of North American Birds*, published in 1983. There may be minor discrepancies, however. Definitions of what distinguishes one species from another can be rather subjective, shifting with the prejudices of tax-onomists. The California Gnatcatcher (*Polioptila californica*) (p.161), for example, was considered a subspecies of the Black-tailed Gnatcatcher (*Polioptila melanura*) until 1989, when, presented with new field evidence, the A.O.U. elevated it to full species status. Keeping up with such changes can be a frustrating and futile exercise, but I have supplied the *Life List* with the A.O.U. classifications current through at least 1992.

In keeping with the belief that birders are concerned about the diminishing biodiversity around them, I have included in the margins the up-to-date status of species listed as Threatened or Endangered under the federal Endangered Species Act. They are distinguished in this book by the symbol ‡. Under this law, subspecies or distinct populations of species receive the same legal protection as full species; this means that in *A Birder's Life List & Journal* a species may be identified as Threatened or Endangered when in fact only a subspecies or particular population has been so designated. In such cases, I have tried to be both precise and clear.

For example, the Canada Goose (*Branta canadensis*) (p.29) is noted as a Threatened species, even though it is common enough in many places to be considered a nuisance. Yet the marginalia specifies that one subspecies, the Aleutian Canada Goose (*B. c. leucopareia*), which nests on islands off Alaska, is in trouble.

As recent controversies such as the one surrounding the Northern Spotted Owl have shown, the listing of endangered species is a political as well as a scientific act. The process of declaring animals and plants endangered, and thereby making them eligible for sometimes costly federal protection, was greatly slowed during the 1980s; as a result, the backlog of candidate species for the Endangered Species List (the grimmest list of all) has grown unfortunately large. The Endangered or Threatened birds highlighted in this book, therefore, should be considered only the official ones. There are, in all likelihood, many more.

It's my wish that *A Bird Lover's Life List & Journal* will be a source of useful information as well as a place where field observations – sex of bird seen, length of sighting, light and weather conditions, behavior – can be easily recorded. Such data, I hope, will be animated by Audubon's stunning prints and, more intimately, by accretions of personal detail, so that in the future a birder wishing to relive any sighting can begin to do so by pulling this volume from the shelf. May this book reveal not only the life of birds, but something about the life of the birder as well.

Norman Boucher

"IN MY SLEEP," AUDUBON WROTE, "I dream continually of birds." An
unsuccessful merchant and investor, he gambled everything on one bold
dream: to paint, life-sized and in poses at once accurate and dramatic,
every North American bird he could find. Versions of these paintings,
engraved on copper plates, would be printed and hand-colored on dou-
ble-elephant pages, 29$^1/_2$ inches wide and 39$^1/_2$ inches tall, the largest
sheets of paper then available. The result would be something new, a
comprehensive joining of science and art. In Florida in 1831, during a
break from wading in search of new birds through mosquito-infested
marshes, he wrote: "I know I am engaged in an arduous undertaking; but
if I live to complete it, I will offer to my country a beautiful monument
of the varied splendour of American nature, and of my devotion to American ornithology."

  The Birds of America, that beautiful monument, was published in London and Edinburgh between 1826 and 1838. It consisted of 435 reproductions bound in four massive, leather-bound volumes. Fewer than 200 sets
were produced, each selling for a $1,000 subscription. Audubon's gamble,
for the most part, had worked. The combination of splendor and ornithology did not exactly make him wealthy – his wife was poor enough ten
years after his death to sell his own set
for $600, and a few years after that, to
sell the original watercolors for $4,000
– but the work did bring him the fame
and respectability that had eluded him
for much of his life.

  It was respectability, the sense of a
secure persona respected by the com-
munity at large, that came hardest to this complex, elusive man. He was
born Jean Rabine on April 26, 1785, the illegitimate son of a French
chambermaid on Santo Domingo (now the Republic of Haiti) and of
Jean Audubon, a French sea captain and slave trader with a plantation on
the island and a wife back in France. When young Jean's mother died less
than seven months after his birth, the boy was raised by another of his
father's mistresses, this one of mixed French and African blood. Five years
later the captain returned to France, where his wife adopted the boy and
had him christened Jean Jacques Fougère Audubon.

  In 1803, dodging Napoleon's draft, 18-year-old Jean Jacques anglicized
his name to John James and moved to Mill Grove, an estate his father
owned near Valley Forge, Pennsylvania. He soon married Lucy Bakewell,
the daughter of a neighboring English gentleman, and proceeded to fail
miserably at business, so miserably that in 1819 he was jailed briefly for
unpaid debts. Meanwhile his passion for drawing and nature flourished.
So did his imagined idea of himself. He reinvented his birth, fabricating

ABOUT
AUDUBON

an operatic story of his father's marriage to a beautiful and wealthy Spanish woman along the Mississippi River in Louisiana, and her subsequent murder on Santo Domingo by blacks in revolt. He began referring to himself as LaForest. Eventually the legend sprang up that he was the Lost Dauphin, son of Louis XVI and Marie Antoinette.

All the while he studied birds, watching them, shooting them, drawing them. "I have a rival in every bird," Lucy confided to her sister. Despite praise from ornithologists, he was unable to find a publisher for his watercolors in the United States. Undaunted, he went to Europe. In Edinburgh, he won the spirited support of the engraver William Lizars, and later, when Lizars had to abandon the project after completing only ten plates, Audubon had the good fortune to find Robert Havell, Jr., whose magnificent engravings (some reproduced in these pages) capture both the drama and the delicacy of Audubon's inclusive vision.

Wherever he went, Audubon solicited subscriptions to support the *The Birds of America*. He modified his persona to fit the expectations of potential subscribers, metamorphosing when needed from buckskin-clad American woodsman to silk-stockinged sophisticate. Strong-featured, he stood five feet ten inches tall, "with muscles of steel," and was particularly vain about his long, "flowing" hair. Walking in cities, he noticed women noticing him.

Yet he was happiest stalking birds through swamps, down rivers, into forests. Back working "like a cart horse" in the New World, he traveled from the Tortugas to Labrador, shooting birds by the dozens, then wiring the best of them into animated poses, and drawing them before the color dulled in their feathers. He discovered species new to science, and defended the precision of his observations against skeptics who thought he exaggerated fact for the sake of drama.

Respectability had come at last, and when he steamed up the Missouri to the mouth of the Yellowstone at the age of 58, he went as a famous and remarkable man. But some of the old zest was gone, and in the end his decline was swift and sad. He continued to work at his home on the Hudson until his eyes went bad. By the late 1840s, he was senile. "His is indeed a most melancholy case," wrote his friend John Bachman when he visited Audubon in 1848. "The outlines of his countenance & his general robust form are there, but the mind is all in ruins." He died on January 27, 1851, and was buried in the cemetery at Trinity Church in upper Manhattan. His hair, his great pride, still flowed to his shoulders, but it had turned white, like feathers on the head of an eagle.

Red-throated Loon *Gavia stellata*

DATE   ☐ *seen*   ☐ *heard*

LOCATION

HABITAT

REMARKS

Arctic Loon *Gavia arctica*

DATE   ☐ *seen*   ☐ *heard*

LOCATION

HABITAT

REMARKS

In his journal, Audubon describes his son and a friend "tolling" for loons, "hallooing and waving a handkerchief" to draw them near: "This 'tolling' is curious and wonderful. Many other species of water-fowl are deceived by these manoeuvres, but none so completely as the Loon."

Pacific Loon *Gavia pacifica*

DATE   ☐ *seen*   ☐ *heard*

LOCATION

HABITAT

REMARKS

Common Loon *Gavia immer*

DATE   ☐ *seen*   ☐ *heard*

LOCATION

HABITAT

REMARKS

Yellow-billed Loon   *Gavia adamsii*

DATE   ☐ *seen*   ☐ *heard*

LOCATION

HABITAT

REMARKS

GREBES   *Podicipedidae*

PODICIPEDIFORMES

Least Grebe   *Tachybaptus dominicus*

DATE   ☐ *seen*   ☐ *heard*

LOCATION

HABITAT

REMARKS

Pied-billed Grebe   *Podilymbus podiceps*

DATE   ☐ *seen*   ☐ *heard*

LOCATION

HABITAT

REMARKS

"Few birds plunge with more rapidity," Audubon wrote of the Pied-billed Grebe. "While submerged it uses its wings to propel itself, as I once saw when some of them passed under a boat in which I was pursuing them."

Horned Grebe   *Podiceps auritus*

DATE   ☐ *seen*   ☐ *heard*

LOCATION

HABITAT

REMARKS

Red-necked Grebe · *Podiceps grisegena*

DATE   ☐ *seen*   ☐ *heard*

LOCATION

HABITAT

REMARKS

Eared Grebe · *Podiceps nigricollis*

DATE   ☐ *seen*   ☐ *heard*

LOCATION

HABITAT

REMARKS

Western Grebe · *Aechmophorus occidentalis*

DATE   ☐ *seen*   ☐ *heard*

LOCATION

HABITAT

REMARKS

Clark's Grebe · *Aechmophorus clarkii*

DATE   ☐ *seen*   ☐ *heard*

LOCATION

HABITAT

REMARKS

Albatrosses, among the longest-lived birds in the wild, can reach 40 years of age or more, sometimes outlasting the bands that scientists attach to their feet to keep track of them.

Short-tailed Albatross   *Diomedea albatrus*

DATE _____   ☐ *seen*   ☐ *heard*

LOCATION _____

HABITAT _____

REMARKS _____

_____

_____

Black-footed Albatross   *Diomedea nigripes*

DATE _____   ☐ *seen*   ☐ *heard*

LOCATION _____

HABITAT _____

REMARKS _____

_____

_____

Laysan Albatross   *Diomedea immutabilis*

DATE _____   ☐ *seen*   ☐ *heard*

LOCATION _____

HABITAT _____

REMARKS _____

_____

_____

Yellow-nosed Albatross   *Diomedea chlororhynchos*

DATE _____   ☐ *seen*   ☐ *heard*

LOCATION _____

HABITAT _____

REMARKS _____

_____

_____

Northern Fulmar   *Fulmarus glacialis*

DATE   ☐ *seen*   ☐ *heard*

LOCATION

HABITAT

REMARKS

Black-capped Petrel   *Pterodroma hasitata*

DATE   ☐ *seen*   ☐ *heard*

LOCATION

HABITAT

REMARKS

Mottled Petrel   *Pterodroma inexpectata*

DATE   ☐ *seen*   ☐ *heard*

LOCATION

HABITAT

REMARKS

Cory's Shearwater   *Calonectris diomedea*

DATE   ☐ *seen*   ☐ *heard*

LOCATION

HABITAT

REMARKS

Pink-footed Shearwater   *Puffinus creatopus*

DATE   □ *seen*   □ *heard*

LOCATION

HABITAT

REMARKS

Flesh-footed Shearwater   *Puffinus carneipes*

DATE   □ *seen*   □ *heard*

LOCATION

HABITAT

REMARKS

Greater Shearwater   *Puffinus gravis*

DATE   □ *seen*   □ *heard*

LOCATION

HABITAT

REMARKS

Buller's Shearwater   *Puffinus bulleri*

DATE   □ *seen*   □ *heard*

LOCATION

HABITAT

REMARKS

Sooty Shearwater   *Puffinus griseus*

DATE   ☐ *seen*   ☐ *heard*

LOCATION

HABITAT

REMARKS

Short-tailed Shearwater   *Puffinus tenuirostris*

DATE   ☐ *seen*   ☐ *heard*

LOCATION

HABITAT

REMARKS

Manx Shearwater   *Puffinus puffinus*

DATE   ☐ *seen*   ☐ *heard*

LOCATION

HABITAT

REMARKS

Black-vented Shearwater   *Puffinus opisthomelas*

DATE   ☐ *seen*   ☐ *heard*

LOCATION

HABITAT

REMARKS

Although Audubon named dozens of North American birds, many after friends, only the Audubon's Shearwater and the Audubon's Oriole commemorate him in their common names.

Audubon's Shearwater   *Puffinus lherminieri*

DATE   ☐ *seen*   ☐ *heard*

LOCATION

HABITAT

REMARKS

STORM-PETRELS   *Hydrobatidae*

Wilson's Storm-Petrel   *Oceanites oceanicus*

DATE   ☐ *seen*   ☐ *heard*

LOCATION

HABITAT

REMARKS

White-faced Storm-Petrel   *Pelagodroma marina*

DATE   ☐ *seen*   ☐ *heard*

LOCATION

HABITAT

REMARKS

Fork-tailed Storm-Petrel   *Oceanodroma furcata*

DATE   ☐ *seen*   ☐ *heard*

LOCATION

HABITAT

REMARKS

Leach's Storm-Petrel *Oceanodroma leucorhoa*

DATE ☐ *seen* ☐ *heard*

LOCATION

HABITAT

REMARKS

Ashy Storm-Petrel *Oceanodroma homochroa*

DATE ☐ *seen* ☐ *heard*

LOCATION

HABITAT

REMARKS

Band-rumped Storm-Petrel *Oceanodroma castro*

DATE ☐ *seen* ☐ *heard*

LOCATION

HABITAT

REMARKS

Black Storm-Petrel *Oceanodroma melania*

DATE ☐ *seen* ☐ *heard*

LOCATION

HABITAT

REMARKS

STORM-PETRELS *Hydrobatidae*

Least Storm-Petrel | *Oceanodroma microsoma*

DATE | ☐ *seen* ☐ *heard*

LOCATION

HABITAT

REMARKS

TROPICBIRDS *Phaethontida*

White-tailed Tropicbird | *Phaethon lepturus*

DATE | ☐ *seen* ☐ *heard*

LOCATION

HABITAT

REMARKS

Red-billed Tropicbird | *Phaethon aethereus*

DATE | ☐ *seen* ☐ *heard*

LOCATION

HABITAT

REMARKS

BOOBIES AND GANNETS *Sulidae*

Masked Booby | *Sula dactylatra*

DATE | ☐ *seen* ☐ *heard*

LOCATION

HABITAT

REMARKS

Blue-footed Booby   *Sula nebouxii*

DATE   ☐ *seen*   ☐ *heard*

LOCATION

HABITAT

REMARKS

Brown Booby   *Sula leucogaster*

DATE   ☐ *seen*   ☐ *heard*

LOCATION

HABITAT

REMARKS

Of the Brown Booby, Audubon wrote: "I am unable to find a good reason for this Gannet's having been called the *Booby*. Authors, it is true, generally represent them as extremely stupid, but to me the word is utterly inapplicable to any bird with which I am acquainted."

Red-footed Booby   *Sula sula*

DATE   ☐ *seen*   ☐ *heard*

LOCATION

HABITAT

REMARKS

Northern Gannet   *Morus bassanus*

DATE   ☐ *seen*   ☐ *heard*

LOCATION

HABITAT

REMARKS

Brown Pelican (PLATE CCLI)

American White Pelican   *Pelecanus erythrorhynchos*

DATE   ☐ *seen*   ☐ *heard*

LOCATION

HABITAT

REMARKS

Brown Pelican‡   *Pelecanus occidentalis*

DATE   ☐ *seen*   ☐ *heard*

LOCATION

HABITAT

REMARKS

‡ENDANGERED In 1903 Pelican Island, a Brown Pelican colony in Florida's Indian River, became the nation's first federal wildlife refuge. Since then, populations in Florida have bounced back, but the species remains endangered along the Pacific and Gulf coasts. Audubon nicknamed these birds The Reverend Sirs.

CORMORANTS   *Phalacrocoracidae*

Great Cormorant   *Phalacrocorax carbo*

DATE   ☐ *seen*   ☐ *heard*

LOCATION

HABITAT

REMARKS

Double-crested Cormorant   *Phalacrocorax auritus*

DATE   ☐ *seen*   ☐ *heard*

LOCATION

HABITAT

REMARKS

Neotropic Cormorant   *Phalacrocorax brasilianus*

DATE   ☐ *seen*   ☐ *heard*

LOCATION

HABITAT

REMARKS

Brandt's Cormorant   *Phalacrocorax penicillatus*

DATE   ☐ *seen*   ☐ *heard*

LOCATION

HABITAT

REMARKS

Pelagic Cormorant   *Phalacrocorax pelagicus*

DATE   ☐ *seen*   ☐ *heard*

LOCATION

HABITAT

REMARKS

Red-faced Cormorant   *Phalacrocorax urile*

DATE   ☐ *seen*   ☐ *heard*

LOCATION

HABITAT

REMARKS

Anhinga *Anhinga anhinga*

DATE ☐ *seen* ☐ *heard*

LOCATION

HABITAT

REMARKS

Magnificent Frigatebird *Fregata magnificens*

DATE ☐ *seen* ☐ *heard*

LOCATION

HABITAT

REMARKS

"There he floats in the pure air, but thither can fancy alone follow him," Audubon wrote of the flight of the Magnificent Frigatebird. "Would that I could accompany him!"

American Bittern *Botaurus lentiginosus*

DATE ☐ *seen* ☐ *heard*

LOCATION

HABITAT

REMARKS

CICONIIFORMES

According to Audubon, the watercolor on which the plate of the American Bittern is based was painted by his son John Woodhouse Audubon.

Least Bittern *Ixobrychus exilis*

DATE ☐ *seen* ☐ *heard*

LOCATION

HABITAT

REMARKS

"But now, he moves; he has taken a silent step, and with great care he advances; slowly does he raise his head from his shoulders, and now, what a sudden start! His formidable bill has transfixed a perch, which he beats to death on the ground."(Audubon on the Great Blue Heron)

Great Blue Heron	*Ardea herodias*
DATE	☐ *seen* ☐ *heard*
LOCATION	
HABITAT	
REMARKS	

American Bittern (PLATE CCCXXXVII)

Great Egret   *Casmerodius albus*

DATE   ☐ *seen*   ☐ *heard*

LOCATION

HABITAT

REMARKS

Snowy Egret   *Egretta thula*

DATE   ☐ *seen*   ☐ *heard*

LOCATION

HABITAT

REMARKS

Little Blue Heron   *Egretta caerulea*

DATE   ☐ *seen*   ☐ *heard*

LOCATION

HABITAT

REMARKS

Tricolored Heron   *Egretta tricolor*

DATE   ☐ *seen*   ☐ *heard*

LOCATION

HABITAT

REMARKS

"I never see this interesting Heron, without calling it the Lady of the Waters."(Audubon on the Tricolored Heron)

Great Blue Heron (PLATE CCXI)

Snowy Egret (Snowy Heron, PLATE CCXLII)

Reddish Egret	*Egretta rufescens*
DATE	☐ *seen* ☐ *heard*
LOCATION	
HABITAT	
REMARKS	

Although common today, the Cattle Egret was unknown in North America during Audubon's time. A native of Africa, it was not found in Florida until the early 1940s.

Cattle Egret	*Bubulcus ibis*
DATE	☐ *seen* ☐ *heard*
LOCATION	
HABITAT	
REMARKS	

Green-backed Heron	*Butorides striatus*
DATE	☐ *seen* ☐ *heard*
LOCATION	
HABITAT	
REMARKS	

Black-crowned Night-Heron	*Nycticorax nycticorax*
DATE	☐ *seen* ☐ *heard*
LOCATION	
HABITAT	
REMARKS	

Yellow-crowned Night-Heron   *Nyctanassa violacea*

DATE   ☐ *seen*   ☐ *heard*

LOCATION

HABITAT

REMARKS

White Ibis   *Eudocimus albus*

DATE   ☐ *seen*   ☐ *heard*

LOCATION

HABITAT

REMARKS

When Audubon tried to collect a White Ibis he had shot late one summer, an alligator almost beat him to the wounded bird. After shooting the alligator, Audubon felt so sorry for the terrified ibis that he nursed it back to health over the winter and released it the following spring.

Glossy Ibis   *Plegadis falcinellus*

DATE   ☐ *seen*   ☐ *heard*

LOCATION

HABITAT

REMARKS

Audubon on his print of the Glossy Ibis: "I have given the figure of a male bird in superb plumage, procured in Florida, near a wood-cutter's cabin, a view of which is also given."

White-faced Ibis   *Plegadis chihi*

DATE   ☐ *seen*   ☐ *heard*

LOCATION

HABITAT

REMARKS

Like the egrets, the Roseate
Spoonbill was among the
species most devastated by the
trade in millinery plumes that
flourished at the turn of the
century. Abundant once more,
it now must survive the alter-
ation of much of its wetland
habitat.

Roseate Spoonbill	*Ajaia ajaja*
DATE	☐ *seen* ☐ *heard*
LOCATION	
HABITAT	
REMARKS	

Black-crowned Night-Heron (Night Heron or Qua Bird, PLATE CCXXXVI)

Wood Stork ‡   *Mycteria americana*

DATE   ☐ *seen*   ☐ *heard*

LOCATION

HABITAT

REMARKS

‡ENDANGERED The number of Wood Storks nesting in Everglades National Park has dropped 80 percent since the 1960s, as urban and agricultural development has ravaged the landscape of south Florida.

Glossy Ibis (PLATE CCCLXXXVII)

" . . . although I saw a great number of them in the course of my stay in that country," Audubon wrote of the Greater Flamingos he found in the Florida Keys, "I cannot even at this moment boast of having had the satisfaction of shooting a single individual."

Greater Flamingo   *Phoenicopterus ruber*

DATE   ☐ *seen*   ☐ *heard*

LOCATION

HABITAT

REMARKS

ANSERIFORMES

Believed to be declining on its nesting grounds in southern California and Arizona, the Southwest population of the Fulvous Whistling-Duck is under consideration for addition to the federal Endangered Species List.

SWANS, GEESE, & DUCKS   *Anatidae*

Fulvous Whistling-Duck   *Dendrocygna bicolor*

DATE   ☐ *seen*   ☐ *heard*

LOCATION

HABITAT

REMARKS

Black-bellied Whistling-Duck   *Dendrocygna autumnalis*

DATE   ☐ *seen*   ☐ *heard*

LOCATION

HABITAT

REMARKS

Tundra Swan   *Cygnus columbianus*

DATE   ☐ *seen*   ☐ *heard*

LOCATION

HABITAT

REMARKS

Greater Flamingo (American Flamingo, PLATE CCCCXXXI)

Whooper Swan   *Cygnus cygnus*

DATE   ☐ *seen*   ☐ *heard*

LOCATION

HABITAT

REMARKS

One day in 1810, Audubon went on a Trumpeter Swan shoot with a group of Shawnees. "I saw these beautiful birds floating on the water," he wrote, "their backs downwards, their heads under the surface, and their legs in the air, struggling in the last agonies of life, to the number of at least 50 – their beautiful skins all intended for the ladies of Europe."

Trumpeter Swan   *Cygnus buccinator*

DATE   ☐ *seen*   ☐ *heard*

LOCATION

HABITAT

REMARKS

Mute Swan   *Cygnus olor*

DATE   ☐ *seen*   ☐ *heard*

LOCATION

HABITAT

REMARKS

Bean Goose   *Anser fabalis*

DATE   ☐ *seen*   ☐ *heard*

LOCATION

HABITAT

REMARKS

Greater White-fronted Goose   *Anser albifrons*

DATE   ☐ *seen*   ☐ *heard*

LOCATION

HABITAT

REMARKS

Snow Goose   *Chen caerulescens*

DATE   ☐ *seen*   ☐ *heard*

LOCATION

HABITAT

REMARKS

Ross' Goose   *Chen rossii*

DATE   ☐ *seen*   ☐ *heard*

LOCATION

HABITAT

REMARKS

Emperor Goose   *Chen canagica*

DATE   ☐ *seen*   ☐ *heard*

LOCATION

HABITAT

REMARKS

Tundra Swan (Common American Swan, PLATE CCCCXI)

Green-winged Teal (PLATE CCXXVIII)

Brant   *Branta bernicla*

DATE   ☐ *seen*   ☐ *heard*

LOCATION

HABITAT

REMARKS

Barnacle Goose   *Branta leucopsis*

DATE   ☐ *seen*   ☐ *heard*

LOCATION

HABITAT

REMARKS

Canada Goose ‡   *Branta canadensis*

DATE   ☐ *seen*   ☐ *heard*

LOCATION

HABITAT

REMARKS

‡THREATENED The Aleutian subspecies of the Canada Goose, once common off the Alaskan coast and throughout the Bering Sea, was decimated by human introduction of arctic foxes onto their breeding islands. Today there are almost 6,000 Aleutian Canada geese, up from 800 in 1975. The bird is smaller than the familiar and abundant Canada Goose.

Wood Duck   *Aix sponsa*

DATE   ☐ *seen*   ☐ *heard*

LOCATION

HABITAT

REMARKS

"On land, the Green-Wing moves with more ease and grace than any other species I know, except our beautiful Wood Duck." (Audubon on the Green-winged Teal)

Green-winged Teal   *Anas crecca*

DATE   ☐ *seen*   ☐ *heard*

LOCATION

HABITAT

REMARKS

Falcated Teal   *Anas falcata*

DATE   ☐ *seen*   ☐ *heard*

LOCATION

HABITAT

REMARKS

American Black Duck   *Anas rubripes*

DATE   ☐ *seen*   ☐ *heard*

LOCATION

HABITAT

REMARKS

Mottled Duck   *Anas fulvigula*

DATE   ☐ *seen*   ☐ *heard*

LOCATION

HABITAT

REMARKS

Mallard   *Anas platyrhynchos*

DATE   ☐ *seen*   ☐ *heard*

LOCATION

HABITAT

REMARKS

Audubon on the Mallard: "The Duck at home is the descendant of a race of slaves, and has lost his spirit. . . . But the free-born, the untamed Duck of the swamps – see how he springs on the wing and hies himself over the woods."

Northern Pintail   *Anas acuta*

DATE   ☐ *seen*   ☐ *heard*

LOCATION

HABITAT

REMARKS

Garganey   *Anas querquedula*

DATE   ☐ *seen*   ☐ *heard*

LOCATION

HABITAT

REMARKS

Blue-winged Teal   *Anas discors*

DATE   ☐ *seen*   ☐ *heard*

LOCATION

HABITAT

REMARKS

"Their flight is extremely rapid and well sustained," Audubon observed of the Blue-Winged Teal, "possibly equal to that of the Passenger Pigeon. The blue of their wings glistens like polished steel in clear sunny weather."

Cinammon Teal	*Anas cyanoptera*
DATE	☐ *seen* ☐ *heard*
LOCATION	
HABITAT	
REMARKS	

American Wigeon (American Widgeon, PLATE CCCXLV)

Northern Shoveler *Anas clypeata*

DATE ☐ *seen* ☐ *heard*

LOCATION

HABITAT

REMARKS

Gadwall *Anas strepera*

DATE ☐ *seen* ☐ *heard*

LOCATION

HABITAT

REMARKS

Eurasian Wigeon *Anas penelope*

DATE ☐ *seen* ☐ *heard*

LOCATION

HABITAT

REMARKS

American Wigeon *Anas americana*

DATE ☐ *seen* ☐ *heard*

LOCATION

HABITAT

REMARKS

Common Pochard	*Aythya ferina*
DATE	☐ *seen* ☐ *heard*
LOCATION	
HABITAT	
REMARKS	

Blue-winged Teal (PLATE CCCXIII)

Canvasback   *Aythya valisineria*

DATE   ☐ *seen*   ☐ *heard*

LOCATION

HABITAT

REMARKS

Canvasback (Canvas-backed Duck, PLATE CCCI)

Redhead   *Aythya americana*

DATE   ☐ *seen*   ☐ *heard*

LOCATION

HABITAT

REMARKS

Ring-necked Duck   *Aythya collaris*

DATE   ☐ *seen*   ☐ *heard*

LOCATION

HABITAT

REMARKS

Tufted Duck   *Aythya fuligula*

DATE   ☐ *seen*   ☐ *heard*

LOCATION

HABITAT

REMARKS

Greater Scaup   *Aythya marila*

DATE   ☐ *seen*   ☐ *heard*

LOCATION

HABITAT

REMARKS

Lesser Scaup *Aythya affinis*

DATE ☐ *seen* ☐ *heard*

LOCATION

HABITAT

REMARKS

Common Eider *Somateria mollissima*

DATE ☐ *seen* ☐ *heard*

LOCATION

HABITAT

REMARKS

"The comparatively short neck of the Eider, the great expansion of its feet, its flat body, and its exceptional diving power in its search for shell-food set it apart from the other true Ducks."(Audubon on the Common Eider)

King Eider *Somateria spectabilis*

DATE ☐ *seen* ☐ *heard*

LOCATION

HABITAT

REMARKS

Spectacled Eider *Somateria fischeri*

DATE ☐ *seen* ☐ *heard*

LOCATION

HABITAT

REMARKS

Steller's Eider	*Polysticta stelleri*
DATE	☐ *seen* ☐ *heard*
LOCATION	
HABITAT	
REMARKS	

Oldsquaw (Long-tailed Duck, PLATE CCCXII)

Harlequin Duck   *Histrionicus histrionicus*

DATE   ☐ *seen*   ☐ *heard*

LOCATION

HABITAT

REMARKS

Oldsquaw   *Clangula hyemalis*

DATE   ☐ *seen*   ☐ *heard*

LOCATION

HABITAT

REMARKS

Barrow's Goldeneye (Golden-eye Duck, PLATE CCCCIII)

Black Scoter   *Melanitta nigra*

DATE   ☐ *seen*   ☐ *heard*

LOCATION

HABITAT

REMARKS

Surf Scoter   *Melanitta perspicillata*

DATE   ☐ *seen*   ☐ *heard*

LOCATION

HABITAT

REMARKS

White-winged Scoter   *Melanitta fusca*

DATE   ☐ *seen*   ☐ *heard*

LOCATION

HABITAT

REMARKS

"The whistling of its wings may be distinctly heard at a distance of more than half a mile," Audubon wrote of the Common Goldeneye, which was known as the Whistler around his home in Kentucky.

Common Goldeneye   *Bucephala clangula*

DATE   ☐ *seen*   ☐ *heard*

LOCATION

HABITAT

REMARKS

Barrow's Goldeneye   *Bucephala islandica*

DATE   ☐ *seen*   ☐ *heard*

LOCATION

HABITAT

REMARKS

Bufflehead   *Bucephala albeola*

DATE   ☐ *seen*   ☐ *heard*

LOCATION

HABITAT

REMARKS

Smew   *Mergellus albellus*

DATE   ☐ *seen*   ☐ *heard*

LOCATION

HABITAT

REMARKS

Hooded Merganser   *Lophodytes cucullatus*

DATE   ☐ *seen*   ☐ *heard*

LOCATION

HABITAT

REMARKS

Common Merganser	*Mergus merganser*
DATE	☐ *seen* ☐ *heard*
LOCATION	
HABITAT	
REMARKS	

Bufflehead (Buffel-headed Duck, PLATE CCCXXV)

Red-breasted Merganser   *Mergus serrator*

DATE   ☐ *seen*   ☐ *heard*

LOCATION

HABITAT

REMARKS

Common Merganser (Goosander, PLATE CCCXXXI)

"I have found this species hard to kill," Audubon wrote of the Ruddy Duck, "and when wounded very tenacious of life, swimming and diving at times to the last gasp."

Ruddy Duck   *Oxyura jamaicensis*

DATE   ☐ *seen*   ☐ *heard*

LOCATION

HABITAT

REMARKS

Masked Duck   *Oxyura dominica*

DATE   ☐ *seen*   ☐ *heard*

LOCATION

HABITAT

REMARKS

NEW WORLD VULTURES   *Cathartidae*

Black Vulture   *Coragyps atratus*

DATE   ☐ *seen*   ☐ *heard*

LOCATION

HABITAT

REMARKS

Turkey Vulture   *Cathartes aura*

DATE   ☐ *seen*   ☐ *heard*

LOCATION

HABITAT

REMARKS

California Condor‡   *Gymnogyps californianus*

DATE	☐ *seen*	☐ *heard*
LOCATION		
HABITAT		
REMARKS		

‡ENDANGERED   The last wild California Condor was captured on Easter Sunday, 1987. After an expensive and controversial captive breeding program, two zoo-bred birds were released in Ventura County, California, in the fall of 1991.

Osprey   *Pandion haliaetus*

DATE	☐ *seen*	☐ *heard*
LOCATION		
HABITAT		
REMARKS		

Hook-billed Kite   *Chondrohierax uncinatus*

DATE	☐ *seen*	☐ *heard*
LOCATION		
HABITAT		
REMARKS		

American Swallow-tailed Kite   *Elanoides forficatus*

DATE	☐ *seen*	☐ *heard*
LOCATION		
HABITAT		
REMARKS		

Osprey (Fish Hawk, PLATE LXXXI)

Black-shouldered Kite　　*Elanus caeruleus*

DATE　　　　　□ *seen*　□ *heard*

LOCATION

HABITAT

REMARKS

Snail Kite ‡　　*Rostrhamus sociabilis*

DATE　　　　　□ *seen*　□ *heard*

LOCATION

HABITAT

REMARKS

‡ENDANGERED Survival of the rare Everglade Snail Kite, the only subspecies of Snail Kite found in the U.S., is in the hands of water managers in south Florida. The kite's sole food is the freshwater apple snail.

Mississippi Kite　　*Ictinia mississippiensis*

DATE　　　　　□ *seen*　□ *heard*

LOCATION

HABITAT

REMARKS

Bald Eagle ‡　　*Haliaeetus leucocephalus*

DATE　　　　　□ *seen*　□ *heard*

LOCATION

HABITAT

REMARKS

‡ENDANGERED & THREATENED Although officially endangered in most of the lower 48 states, the Bald Eagle, like the Osprey, has recovered well from the ravages of the pesticide DDT. Populations in some northern states have been re-classified as threatened, and others are likely to follow.

Northern Harrier — *Circus cyaneus*

DATE _____ □ *seen*   □ *heard*

LOCATION _____

HABITAT _____

REMARKS _____

_____

Sharp-shinned Hawk — *Accipiter striatus*

DATE _____ □ *seen*   □ *heard*

LOCATION _____

HABITAT _____

REMARKS _____

_____

Cooper's Hawk — *Accipiter cooperii*

DATE _____ □ *seen*   □ *heard*

LOCATION _____

HABITAT _____

REMARKS _____

_____

Several recent studies have concluded that the Northern Goshawk is on the decline, perhaps because of logging and forest management practices. The species is being reviewed for possible Endangered or Threatened designation.

Northern Goshawk — *Accipiter gentilis*

DATE _____ □ *seen*   □ *heard*

LOCATION _____

HABITAT _____

REMARKS _____

_____

Common Black-Hawk *Buteogallus anthracinus*

DATE ☐ *seen* ☐ *heard*

LOCATION

HABITAT

REMARKS

Harris' Hawk *Parabuteo unicinctus*

DATE ☐ *seen* ☐ *heard*

LOCATION

HABITAT

REMARKS

Gray Hawk *Buteo nitidus*

DATE ☐ *seen* ☐ *heard*

LOCATION

HABITAT

REMARKS

Red-shouldered Hawk *Buteo lineatus*

DATE ☐ *seen* ☐ *heard*

LOCATION

HABITAT

REMARKS

Broad-winged Hawk   *Buteo platypterus*

DATE   ☐ *seen*   ☐ *heard*

LOCATION

HABITAT

REMARKS

Short-tailed Hawk   *Buteo brachyurus*

DATE   ☐ *seen*   ☐ *heard*

LOCATION

HABITAT

REMARKS

Swainson's Hawk   *Buteo swainsoni*

DATE   ☐ *seen*   ☐ *heard*

LOCATION

HABITAT

REMARKS

White-tailed Hawk   *Buteo albicaudatus*

DATE   ☐ *seen*   ☐ *heard*

LOCATION

HABITAT

REMARKS

Red-shouldered Hawk (PLATE LVI)

Zone-tailed Hawk   *Buteo albonotatus*

DATE   □ *seen*   □ *heard*

LOCATION

HABITAT

REMARKS

Red-tailed Hawk   *Buteo jamaicensis*

DATE   □ *seen*   □ *heard*

LOCATION

HABITAT

REMARKS

Ferruginous Hawk   *Buteo regalis*

DATE   □ *seen*   □ *heard*

LOCATION

HABITAT

REMARKS

Rough-legged Hawk   *Buteo lagopus*

DATE   □ *seen*   □ *heard*

LOCATION

HABITAT

REMARKS

Golden Eagle   *Aquila chrysaetos*

DATE   ☐ *seen*   ☐ *heard*

LOCATION

HABITAT

REMARKS

FALCONS   *Falconidae*

Crested Caracara‡   *Polyborus plancus*

DATE   ☐ *seen*   ☐ *heard*

LOCATION

HABITAT

REMARKS

‡THREATENED The Crested Caracara was classified as Threatened in 1987, a result of habitat loss in Florida. This U.S. subspecies, *Polyborus plancus audubonii*, bears Audubon's name.

American Kestrel   *Falco sparverius*

DATE   ☐ *seen*   ☐ *heard*

LOCATION

HABITAT

REMARKS

Merlin   *Falco columbarius*

DATE   ☐ *seen*   ☐ *heard*

LOCATION

HABITAT

REMARKS

‡ENDANGERED The North American subspecies of the Aplomado Falcon has been extirpated from the U.S. and is declining in Mexico. Its last hope is a captive breeding and reintroduction program.

Aplomado Falcon ‡   *Falco femoralis*

DATE   ☐ *seen*   ☐ *heard*

LOCATION

HABITAT

REMARKS

Prairie Falcon   *Falco mexicanus*

DATE   ☐ *seen*   ☐ *heard*

LOCATION

HABITAT

REMARKS

‡ ENDANGERED & THREAT-ENED A victim of the pesticide DDT, the Peregrine Falcon was one of the first species listed under the 1973 Endangered Species Act. Today the American subspecies is listed as Endangered, while the Arctic race is Threatened. Thanks to one of one of the most successful endangered species projects ever undertaken, the bird will likely be off the Endangered Species List by the century's end.

Peregrine Falcon ‡   *Falco peregrinus*

DATE   ☐ *seen*   ☐ *heard*

LOCATION

HABITAT

REMARKS

Gyrfalcon   *Falco rusticolus*

DATE   ☐ *seen*   ☐ *heard*

LOCATION

HABITAT

REMARKS

Plain Chachalaca   Ortalis vetula

DATE   ☐ *seen*   ☐ *heard*

LOCATION

HABITAT

REMARKS

PHEASANTS, GROUSE, & QUAILS   *Phasianidae*

Gray Partridge   *Perdix perdix*

DATE   ☐ *seen*   ☐ *heard*

LOCATION

HABITAT

REMARKS

Black Francolin   *Francolinus francolinus*

DATE   ☐ *seen*   ☐ *heard*

LOCATION

HABITAT

REMARKS

Chukar   *Alectoris chukar*

DATE   ☐ *seen*   ☐ *heard*

LOCATION

HABITAT

REMARKS

Ring-necked Pheasant   *Phasianus colchicus*

DATE   ☐ *seen*   ☐ *heard*

LOCATION

HABITAT

REMARKS

Spruce Grouse   *Dendragapus canadensis*

DATE   ☐ *seen*   ☐ *heard*

LOCATION

HABITAT

REMARKS

Blue Grouse   *Dendragapus obscurus*

DATE   ☐ *seen*   ☐ *heard*

LOCATION

HABITAT

REMARKS

Willow Ptarmigan   *Lagopus lagopus*

DATE   ☐ *seen*   ☐ *heard*

LOCATION

HABITAT

REMARKS

Willow Ptarmigan (Willow Grous or Large Ptarmigan, PLATE CXCI)

Rock Ptarmigan   *Lagopus mutus*

DATE   □ *seen*   □ *heard*

LOCATION

HABITAT

REMARKS

White-tailed Ptarmigan   *Lagopus leucurus*

DATE   □ *seen*   □ *heard*

LOCATION

HABITAT

REMARKS

Ruffed Grouse   *Bonasa umbellus*

DATE   □ *seen*   □ *heard*

LOCATION

HABITAT

REMARKS

Sage Grouse   *Centrocercus urophasianus*

DATE   □ *seen*   □ *heard*

LOCATION

HABITAT

REMARKS

Greater Prairie-Chicken‡   *Tympanuchus cupido*

DATE _____   □ *seen*   □ *heard*

LOCATION _____

HABITAT _____

REMARKS _____

Lesser Prairie-Chicken   *Tympanuchus pallidicinctus*

DATE _____   □ *seen*   □ *heard*

LOCATION _____

HABITAT _____

REMARKS _____

Sharp-tailed Grouse   *Tympanuchus phasianellus*

DATE _____   □ *seen*   □ *heard*

LOCATION _____

HABITAT _____

REMARKS _____

Wild Turkey   *Meleagris gallopavo*

DATE _____   □ *seen*   □ *heard*

LOCATION _____

HABITAT _____

REMARKS _____

‡ENDANGERED Attwater's Prairie-Chicken, a Texas subspecies of the Greater Prairie-Chicken, could go extinct early next century. Agriculture and cattle ranching have taken over its native-prairie habitat. Fewer than 500 birds remain, down from about a million a century ago.

Montezuma Quail   *Cyrtonyx montezumae*

DATE   ☐ *seen*   ☐ *heard*

LOCATION

HABITAT

REMARKS

‡ENDANGERED The Masked Bobwhite, a subspecies of the Northern Bobwhite, may be saved from extinction in the U.S. by a reintroduction program in progress on the Buenos Aires National Wildlife Refuge in southern Arizona. Overgrazing by cattle has destroyed much of its original habitat.

Northern Bobwhite ‡   *Colinus virginianus*

DATE   ☐ *seen*   ☐ *heard*

LOCATION

HABITAT

REMARKS

Scaled Quail   *Callipepla squamata*

DATE   ☐ *seen*   ☐ *heard*

LOCATION

HABITAT

REMARKS

Gambel's Quail   *Callipepla gambelii*

DATE   ☐ *seen*   ☐ *heard*

LOCATION

HABITAT

REMARKS

California Quail | *Callipepla californica*

DATE | ☐ *seen* ☐ *heard*

LOCATION

HABITAT

REMARKS

Mountain Quail | *Oreortyx pictus*

DATE | ☐ *seen* ☐ *heard*

LOCATION

HABITAT

REMARKS

RAILS, GALLINULES, & COOTS *Rallidae* GRUIFORMES

Yellow Rail | *Coturnicops noveboracensis*

DATE | ☐ *seen* ☐ *heard*

LOCATION

HABITAT

REMARKS

Black Rail | *Laterallus jamaicensis*

DATE | ☐ *seen* ☐ *heard*

LOCATION

HABITAT

REMARKS

‡ENDANGERED Three western subspecies of the Clapper Rail are endangered, a result of shrinking wetlands. Two are found in California, one in central Arizona. One southern California race, the Light-footed Clapper Rail, is particularly close to extinction and declining.

Clapper Rail ‡   *Rallus longirostris*

DATE   ☐ *seen*   ☐ *heard*

LOCATION

HABITAT

REMARKS

King Rail   *Rallus elegans*

DATE   ☐ *seen*   ☐ *heard*

LOCATION

HABITAT

REMARKS

Virginia Rail   *Rallus limicola*

DATE   ☐ *seen*   ☐ *heard*

LOCATION

HABITAT

REMARKS

Sora   *Porzana carolina*

DATE   ☐ *seen*   ☐ *heard*

LOCATION

HABITAT

REMARKS

Purple Gallinule — *Porphyrula martinica*

DATE ☐ *seen* ☐ *heard*

LOCATION

HABITAT

REMARKS

Common Moorhen — *Gallinula chloropus*

DATE ☐ *seen* ☐ *heard*

LOCATION

HABITAT

REMARKS

"On land it walks somewhat like a chicken," Audubon observed of the Common Moorhen, which was known as the Common Gallinule in his time.

American Coot — *Fulica americana*

DATE ☐ *seen* ☐ *heard*

LOCATION

HABITAT

REMARKS

Caribbean Coot — *Fulica caribaea*

DATE ☐ *seen* ☐ *heard*

LOCATION

HABITAT

REMARKS

Sandhill Crane (Hooping Crane, PLATE CCLXI)

LIMPKINS — *Aramidae*

Limpkin *Aramus guarauna*

DATE ☐ *seen* ☐ *heard*

LOCATION

HABITAT

REMARKS

CRANES — *Gruidae*

Sandhill Crane ‡ *Grus canadensis*

DATE ☐ *seen* ☐ *heard*

LOCATION

HABITAT

REMARKS

‡ENDANGERED The resident Mississippi population of the Sandhill Crane is endangered. Future success depends on protecting its savanna habitat. Water diversion projects along the Platte River in Nebraska may be threatening the northern, migratory subspecies.

Whooping Crane ‡ *Grus americana*

DATE ☐ *seen* ☐ *heard*

LOCATION

HABITAT

REMARKS

‡ENDANGERED Saving the Whooping Crane has been one of the most popular yet frustrating ornithological tasks ever undertaken. The current goal is to increase the wild population, once down to fewer than 12 nesting pairs, up to 90 pairs by 2020. There are plans to one day reintroduce the bird to Florida.

CHARADRIIFORMES

PLOVERS — *Charadriidae*

Northern Lapwing *Vanellus vanellus*

DATE ☐ *seen* ☐ *heard*

LOCATION

HABITAT

REMARKS

Black-bellied Plover   *Pluvialis squatarola*

DATE   ☐ *seen*   ☐ *heard*

LOCATION

HABITAT

REMARKS

Lesser Golden-Plover   *Pluvialis dominica*

DATE   ☐ *seen*   ☐ *heard*

LOCATION

HABITAT

REMARKS

Mongolian Plover   *Charadrius mongolus*

DATE   ☐ *seen*   ☐ *heard*

LOCATION

HABITAT

REMARKS

The subspecies of Snowy Plover found on the beaches of the West coast has been proposed for Threatened status. Fewer than 1,500 birds remain.

Snowy Plover   *Charadrius alexandrinus*

DATE   ☐ *seen*   ☐ *heard*

LOCATION

HABITAT

REMARKS

Wilson's Plover	*Charadrius wilsonia*
DATE	☐ *seen* ☐ *heard*
LOCATION	
HABITAT	
REMARKS	

Common Ringed Plover	*Charadrius hiaticula*
DATE	☐ *seen* ☐ *heard*
LOCATION	
HABITAT	
REMARKS	

Semipalmated Plover	*Charadrius semipalmatus*
DATE	☐ *seen* ☐ *heard*
LOCATION	
HABITAT	
REMARKS	

Piping Plover ‡	*Charadrius melodus*
DATE	☐ *seen* ☐ *heard*
LOCATION	
HABITAT	
REMARKS	

‡ ENDANGERED & THREAT-ENED Piping Plover nesting habitat has given way to condos and vacation homes along the Atlantic coast and Midwestern lakeshores. The entire species has been listed as threatened since late 1985, except for populations around the Great Lakes, which are endangered.

Killdeer   *Charadrius vociferus*

DATE   ☐ *seen*   ☐ *heard*

LOCATION

HABITAT

REMARKS

Mountain Plover   *Charadrius montanus*

DATE   ☐ *seen*   ☐ *heard*

LOCATION

HABITAT

REMARKS

American Avocet (PLATE CCCXVIII)

Eurasian Dotterel — *Charadrius morinellus*

DATE ☐ *seen* ☐ *heard*

LOCATION

HABITAT

REMARKS

American Oystercatcher — *Haematopus palliatus*

DATE ☐ *seen* ☐ *heard*

LOCATION

HABITAT

REMARKS

Black Oystercatcher — *Haematopus bachmani*

DATE ☐ *seen* ☐ *heard*

LOCATION

HABITAT

REMARKS

Black-necked Stilt — *Himantopus mexicanus*

DATE ☐ *seen* ☐ *heard*

LOCATION

HABITAT

REMARKS

American Avocet — *Recurvirostra americana*

DATE   ☐ *seen*   ☐ *heard*

LOCATION

HABITAT

REMARKS

JACANAS — *Jacanidae*

Northern Jacana — *Jacana spinosa*

DATE   ☐ *seen*   ☐ *heard*

LOCATION

HABITAT

REMARKS

SANDPIPERS — *Scolopacidae*

Common Greenshank — *Tringa nebularia*

DATE   ☐ *seen*   ☐ *heard*

LOCATION

HABITAT

REMARKS

Greater Yellowlegs — *Tringa melanoleuca*

DATE   ☐ *seen*   ☐ *heard*

LOCATION

HABITAT

REMARKS

Lesser Yellowlegs	*Tringa flavipes*
DATE	☐ *seen* ☐ *heard*
LOCATION	
HABITAT	
REMARKS	

Spotted Redshank	*Tringa erythropus*
DATE	☐ *seen* ☐ *heard*
LOCATION	
HABITAT	
REMARKS	

Wood Sandpiper	*Tringa glareola*
DATE	☐ *seen* ☐ *heard*
LOCATION	
HABITAT	
REMARKS	

Solitary Sandpiper	*Tringa solitaria*
DATE	☐ *seen* ☐ *heard*
LOCATION	
HABITAT	
REMARKS	

Willet — *Catoptrophorus semipalmatus*

DATE ☐ *seen* ☐ *heard*

LOCATION

HABITAT

REMARKS

Wandering Tattler — *Heteroscelus incanus*

DATE ☐ *seen* ☐ *heard*

LOCATION

HABITAT

REMARKS

Gray-tailed Tattler — *Heteroscelus brevipes*

DATE ☐ *seen* ☐ *heard*

LOCATION

HABITAT

REMARKS

Common Sandpiper — *Actitis hypoleucos*

DATE ☐ *seen* ☐ *heard*

LOCATION

HABITAT

REMARKS

Spotted Sandpiper   *Actitis macularia*

DATE   ☐ *seen*   ☐ *heard*

LOCATION

HABITAT

REMARKS

Upland Sandpiper   *Bartramia longicauda*

DATE   ☐ *seen*   ☐ *heard*

LOCATION

HABITAT

REMARKS

Eskimo Curlew ‡   *Numenius borealis*

DATE   ☐ *seen*   ☐ *heard*

LOCATION

HABITAT

REMARKS

‡ENDANGERED   Once abundant in the far north, migrating Eskimo Curlews were a favorite target of gunners supplying meat for the 19th century market. By 1900 it was virtually extinct, and remains so today.

Whimbrel   *Numenius phaeopus*

DATE   ☐ *seen*   ☐ *heard*

LOCATION

HABITAT

REMARKS

The Bristle-thighed Curlew, thought to be declining, is a candidate for review under the Endangered Species Act.

Bristle-thighed Curlew   *Numenius tahitiensis*

DATE   ☐ *seen*   ☐ *heard*

LOCATION

HABITAT

REMARKS

Long-billed Curlew   *Numenius americanus*

DATE   ☐ *seen*   ☐ *heard*

LOCATION

HABITAT

REMARKS

Black-tailed Godwit   *Limosa limosa*

DATE   ☐ *seen*   ☐ *heard*

LOCATION

HABITAT

REMARKS

Hudsonian Godwit   *Limosa haemastica*

DATE   ☐ *seen*   ☐ *heard*

LOCATION

HABITAT

REMARKS

Bar-tailed Godwit *Limosa lapponica*

DATE ☐ *seen* ☐ *heard*

LOCATION

HABITAT

REMARKS

Marbled Godwit *Limosa fedoa*

DATE ☐ *seen* ☐ *heard*

LOCATION

HABITAT

REMARKS

Ruddy Turnstone *Arenaria interpres*

DATE ☐ *seen* ☐ *heard*

LOCATION

HABITAT

REMARKS

Black Turnstone *Arenaria melanocephala*

DATE ☐ *seen* ☐ *heard*

LOCATION

HABITAT

REMARKS

Surfbird   *Aphriza virgata*

DATE   ☐ *seen*   ☐ *heard*

LOCATION

HABITAT

REMARKS

Red Knot   *Calidris canutus*

DATE   ☐ *seen*   ☐ *heard*

LOCATION

HABITAT

REMARKS

Sanderling   *Calidris alba*

DATE   ☐ *seen*   ☐ *heard*

LOCATION

HABITAT

REMARKS

Semipalmated Sandpiper   *Calidris pusilla*

DATE   ☐ *seen*   ☐ *heard*

LOCATION

HABITAT

REMARKS

Western Sandpiper · *Calidris mauri*

DATE ☐ *seen* ☐ *heard*

LOCATION

HABITAT

REMARKS

Semipalmated Sandpiper (PLATE CCCCV)

Rufous-necked Stint   *Calidris ruficollis*

DATE   ☐ *seen*   ☐ *heard*

LOCATION

HABITAT

REMARKS

Long-toed Stint   *Calidris subminuta*

DATE   ☐ *seen*   ☐ *heard*

LOCATION

HABITAT

REMARKS

While living in Kentucky,
Audubon kept Least Sand-
pipers as pets. He also found
them "tiny, fat, and delicious
birds."

Least Sandpiper   *Calidris minutilla*

DATE   ☐ *seen*   ☐ *heard*

LOCATION

HABITAT

REMARKS

White-rumped Sandpiper   *Calidris fuscicollis*

DATE   ☐ *seen*   ☐ *heard*

LOCATION

HABITAT

REMARKS

Baird's Sandpiper *Calidris bairdii*

DATE ☐ *seen* ☐ *heard*

LOCATION

HABITAT

REMARKS

Pectoral Sandpiper *Calidris melanotos*

DATE ☐ *seen* ☐ *heard*

LOCATION

HABITAT

REMARKS

Sharp-tailed Sandpiper *Calidris acuminata*

DATE ☐ *seen* ☐ *heard*

LOCATION

HABITAT

REMARKS

Purple Sandpiper *Calidris maritima*

DATE ☐ *seen* ☐ *heard*

LOCATION

HABITAT

REMARKS

Rock Sandpiper	*Calidris ptilocnemis*
DATE	☐ *seen* ☐ *heard*
LOCATION	
HABITAT	
REMARKS	

Curlew Sandpiper (Pigmy Curlew, PLATE CCLXIII)

Dunlin   *Calidris alpina*

DATE   ☐ *seen*   ☐ *heard*

LOCATION

HABITAT

REMARKS

Curlew Sandpiper   *Calidris ferruginea*

DATE   ☐ *seen*   ☐ *heard*

LOCATION

HABITAT

REMARKS

Stilt Sandpiper   *Calidris himantopus*

DATE   ☐ *seen*   ☐ *heard*

LOCATION

HABITAT

REMARKS

Buff-breasted Sandpiper   *Tryngites subruficollis*

DATE   ☐ *seen*   ☐ *heard*

LOCATION

HABITAT

REMARKS

Ruff   *Philomachus pugnax*

DATE   ☐ *seen*   ☐ *heard*

LOCATION

HABITAT

REMARKS

Short-billed Dowitcher   *Limnodromus griseus*

DATE   ☐ *seen*   ☐ *heard*

LOCATION

HABITAT

REMARKS

Long-billed Dowitcher   *Limnodromus scolopaceus*

DATE   ☐ *seen*   ☐ *heard*

LOCATION

HABITAT

REMARKS

Common Snipe   *Gallinago gallinago*

DATE   ☐ *seen*   ☐ *heard*

LOCATION

HABITAT

REMARKS

American Woodcock *Scolopax minor*

DATE ☐ *seen* ☐ *heard*

LOCATION

HABITAT

REMARKS

Wilson's Phalarope *Phalaropus tricolor*

DATE ☐ *seen* ☐ *heard*

LOCATION

HABITAT

REMARKS

Red-necked Phalarope *Phalaropus lobatus*

DATE ☐ *seen* ☐ *heard*

LOCATION

HABITAT

REMARKS

Red Phalarope *Phalaropus fulicaria*

DATE ☐ *seen* ☐ *heard*

LOCATION

HABITAT

REMARKS

"I started a Woodcock," Audubon wrote in his journal on May 16, 1843, "and caught one of her young, and I am now sorry for this evil deed." At 58, he was beginning to tire of all his shooting and capturing.

Pomarine Jaeger   *Stercorarius pomarinus*

DATE   ☐ *seen*   ☐ *heard*

LOCATION

HABITAT

REMARKS

Parasitic Jaeger   *Stercorarius parasiticus*

DATE   ☐ *seen*   ☐ *heard*

LOCATION

HABITAT

REMARKS

Long-tailed Jaeger   *Stercorarius longicaudus*

DATE   ☐ *seen*   ☐ *heard*

LOCATION

HABITAT

REMARKS

Great Skua   *Catharacta skua*

DATE   ☐ *seen*   ☐ *heard*

LOCATION

HABITAT

REMARKS

Laughing Gull (Black-headed Gull, PLATE CCCXIV)

South Polar Skua   *Catharacta maccormicki*

DATE   ☐ *seen*   ☐ *heard*

LOCATION

HABITAT

REMARKS

Audubon once observed a Laughing Gull steal a fish from the partially open bill of a Brown Pelican: "The sight of these manoeuvres rendered me almost frantic with delight."

Laughing Gull   *Larus atricilla*

DATE   ☐ *seen*   ☐ *heard*

LOCATION

HABITAT

REMARKS

Franklin's Gull   *Larus pipixcan*

DATE   ☐ *seen*   ☐ *heard*

LOCATION

HABITAT

REMARKS

Little Gull   *Larus minutus*

DATE   ☐ *seen*   ☐ *heard*

LOCATION

HABITAT

REMARKS

Common Black-headed Gull — *Larus ridibundus*

DATE ☐ *seen* ☐ *heard*

LOCATION

HABITAT

REMARKS

Bonaparte's Gull — *Larus philadelphia*

DATE ☐ *seen* ☐ *heard*

LOCATION

HABITAT

REMARKS

Heermann's Gull — *Larus heermanni*

DATE ☐ *seen* ☐ *heard*

LOCATION

HABITAT

REMARKS

Mew Gull — *Larus canus*

DATE ☐ *seen* ☐ *heard*

LOCATION

HABITAT

REMARKS

Ring-billed Gull — *Larus delawarensis*

DATE ☐ *seen* ☐ *heard*

LOCATION

HABITAT

REMARKS

California Gull — *Larus californicus*

DATE ☐ *seen* ☐ *heard*

LOCATION

HABITAT

REMARKS

Herring Gull — *Larus argentatus*

DATE ☐ *seen* ☐ *heard*

LOCATION

HABITAT

REMARKS

Thayer's Gull — *Larus thayeri*

DATE ☐ *seen* ☐ *heard*

LOCATION

HABITAT

REMARKS

Iceland Gull   *Larus glaucoides*

DATE   ☐ *seen*   ☐ *heard*

LOCATION

HABITAT

REMARKS

Lesser Black-backed Gull   *Larus fuscus*

DATE   ☐ *seen*   ☐ *heard*

LOCATION

HABITAT

REMARKS

Slaty-backed Gull   *Larus schistisagus*

DATE   ☐ *seen*   ☐ *heard*

LOCATION

HABITAT

REMARKS

Yellow-footed Gull   *Larus livens*

DATE   ☐ *seen*   ☐ *heard*

LOCATION

HABITAT

REMARKS

Western Gull	*Larus occidentalis*
DATE	☐ *seen* ☐ *heard*
LOCATION	
HABITAT	
REMARKS	

Sabine's Gull & Sanderling (Fork-tailed Gull, PLATE CCLXXXV)

Glaucous-winged Gull   *Larus glaucescens*

DATE   ☐ *seen*   ☐ *heard*

LOCATION

HABITAT

REMARKS

Glaucous Gull   *Larus hyperboreus*

DATE   ☐ *seen*   ☐ *heard*

LOCATION

HABITAT

REMARKS

Great Black-backed Gull   *Larus marinus*

DATE   ☐ *seen*   ☐ *heard*

LOCATION

HABITAT

REMARKS

Of the Great Black-backed Gull, Audubon wrote: "The Great Gull must live an extraordinarily long time, as I have seen one that was kept a captive for more than 30 years."

Black-legged Kittiwake   *Rissa tridactyla*

DATE   ☐ *seen*   ☐ *heard*

LOCATION

HABITAT

REMARKS

Red-legged Kittiwake　　*Rissa brevirostris*

DATE　　　　　□ *seen*　　□ *heard*

LOCATION

HABITAT

REMARKS

Ross' Gull　　*Rhodostethia rosea*

DATE　　　　　□ *seen*　　□ *heard*

LOCATION

HABITAT

REMARKS

Sabine's Gull　　*Xema sabini*

DATE　　　　　□ *seen*　　□ *heard*

LOCATION

HABITAT

REMARKS

Ivory Gull　　*Pagophila eburnea*

DATE　　　　　□ *seen*　　□ *heard*

LOCATION

HABITAT

REMARKS

Gull-billed Tern	*Sterna nilotica*
DATE	☐ *seen* ☐ *heard*
LOCATION	
HABITAT	
REMARKS	

Caspian Tern	*Sterna caspia*
DATE	☐ *seen* ☐ *heard*
LOCATION	
HABITAT	
REMARKS	

Royal Tern	*Sterna maxima*
DATE	☐ *seen* ☐ *heard*
LOCATION	
HABITAT	
REMARKS	

Elegant Tern	*Sterna elegans*
DATE	☐ *seen* ☐ *heard*
LOCATION	
HABITAT	
REMARKS	

Like many terns, the Elegant Tern has suffered from coastal development. It is a candidate for review under the Endangered Species Act.

Sandwich Tern   *Sterna sandvicensis*

DATE   ☐ *seen*   ☐ *heard*

LOCATION

HABITAT

REMARKS

‡ ENDANGERED & THREAT-
ENED Gulls proliferating
alongside human coastal settle-
ments have invaded Roseate
Tern nesting colonies, resulting
in its addition to the federal
Endangered Species List in 1987.
The danger is greatest in the
Northeast, where the tern is
endangered. It is threatened in
Florida.

Roseate Tern ‡   *Sterna dougallii*

DATE   ☐ *seen*   ☐ *heard*

LOCATION

HABITAT

REMARKS

Common Tern   *Sterna hirundo*

DATE   ☐ *seen*   ☐ *heard*

LOCATION

HABITAT

REMARKS

Arctic Tern   *Sterna paradisaea*

DATE   ☐ *seen*   ☐ *heard*

LOCATION

HABITAT

REMARKS

Forster's Tern · *Sterna forsteri*

DATE ☐ *seen* ☐ *heard*

LOCATION

HABITAT

REMARKS

Least Tern ‡ · *Sterna antillarum*

DATE ☐ *seen* ☐ *heard*

LOCATION

HABITAT

REMARKS

‡ENDANGERED The Least Tern has lost nesting colonies to coastal development in California and to channelization and damming along the Missouri, Mississippi, Ohio, Red, and Rio Grande Rivers.

Aleutian Tern · *Sterna aleutica*

DATE ☐ *seen* ☐ *heard*

LOCATION

HABITAT

REMARKS

Bridled Tern · *Sterna anaethetus*

DATE ☐ *seen* ☐ *heard*

LOCATION

HABITAT

REMARKS

The vulnerability of terns is evident from Audubon's report of seamen running through a colony of nesting Sooty Terns, flailing sticks to fend off the diving adults: "In less than half an hour, more than a hundred Terns lay dead in a heap, and a number of baskets were filled to the brim with eggs."

Sooty Tern   *Sterna fuscata*

DATE   ☐ *seen*   ☐ *heard*

LOCATION

HABITAT

REMARKS

White-winged Tern   *Chlidonias leucopterus*

DATE   ☐ *seen*   ☐ *heard*

LOCATION

HABITAT

REMARKS

Black Tern   *Chlidonias niger*

DATE   ☐ *seen*   ☐ *heard*

LOCATION

HABITAT

REMARKS

Brown Noddy   *Anous stolidus*

DATE   ☐ *seen*   ☐ *heard*

LOCATION

HABITAT

REMARKS

Black Noddy	*Anous minutus*
DATE	☐ *seen* ☐ *heard*
LOCATION	
HABITAT	
REMARKS	

Black Skimmer	*Rynchops niger*
DATE	☐ *seen* ☐ *heard*
LOCATION	
HABITAT	
REMARKS	

In Florida, Audubon saw huge flocks of Black Skimmers, "not fewer than 10,000 . . . in a single flock." Their flight, he believed, "is perhaps more elegant than that of any water bird with which I am acquainted."

AUKS	*Alcidae*
Dovekie	*Alle alle*
DATE	☐ *seen* ☐ *heard*
LOCATION	
HABITAT	
REMARKS	

Common Murre	*Uria aalge*
DATE	☐ *seen* ☐ *heard*
LOCATION	
HABITAT	
REMARKS	

Thick-billed Murre   *Uria lomvia*

DATE   ☐ *seen*   ☐ *heard*

LOCATION

HABITAT

REMARKS

Razorbill   *Alca torda*

DATE   ☐ *seen*   ☐ *heard*

LOCATION

HABITAT

REMARKS

Black Guillemot   *Cepphus grylle*

DATE   ☐ *seen*   ☐ *heard*

LOCATION

HABITAT

REMARKS

Pigeon Guillemot   *Cepphus columba*

DATE   ☐ *seen*   ☐ *heard*

LOCATION

HABITAT

REMARKS

Marbled Murrelet   *Brachyramphus marmoratus*

DATE   ☐ *seen*   ☐ *heard*

LOCATION

HABITAT

REMARKS

In early 1992, threatened status was proposed for the Marbled Murrelet, its decline a result of the cutting of old-growth and mature forest, as well as mortality from gill-net fishing and oil spills.

Kittlitz's Murrelet   *Brachyramphus brevirostris*

DATE   ☐ *seen*   ☐ *heard*

LOCATION

HABITAT

REMARKS

Xantus' Murrelet   *Synthliboramphus hypoleucus*

DATE   ☐ *seen*   ☐ *heard*

LOCATION

HABITAT

REMARKS

Craveri's Murrelet   *Synthliboramphus craveri*

DATE   ☐ *seen*   ☐ *heard*

LOCATION

HABITAT

REMARKS

Ancient Murrelet *Synthliboramphus antiquus*

DATE ☐ *seen* ☐ *heard*

LOCATION

HABITAT

REMARKS

Cassin's Auklet *Ptychoramphus aleuticus*

DATE ☐ *seen* ☐ *heard*

LOCATION

HABITAT

REMARKS

Parakeet Auklet *Cyclorrhynchus psittacula*

DATE ☐ *seen* ☐ *heard*

LOCATION

HABITAT

REMARKS

Least Auklet *Aethia pusilla*

DATE ☐ *seen* ☐ *heard*

LOCATION

HABITAT

REMARKS

Whiskered Auklet

Aethia pygmaea

DATE ☐ *seen* ☐ *heard*

LOCATION

HABITAT

REMARKS

Crested Auklet

Aethia cristatella

DATE ☐ *seen* ☐ *heard*

LOCATION

HABITAT

REMARKS

Rhinoceros Auklet

Cerorhinca monocerata

DATE ☐ *seen* ☐ *heard*

LOCATION

HABITAT

REMARKS

Tufted Puffin

Fratercula cirrhata

DATE ☐ *seen* ☐ *heard*

LOCATION

HABITAT

REMARKS

Atlantic Puffin	*Fratercula arctica*
DATE	☐ *seen* ☐ *heard*
LOCATION	
HABITAT	
REMARKS	

Atlantic Puffin (Puffin, PLATE CCXIII)

Horned Puffin   *Fratercula corniculata*

DATE   ☐ *seen*   ☐ *heard*

LOCATION

HABITAT

REMARKS

PIGEONS & DOVES   *Columbidae*   COLUMBIFORMES

Rock Dove   *Columba livia*

DATE   ☐ *seen*   ☐ *heard*

LOCATION

HABITAT

REMARKS

White-crowned Pigeon   *Columba leucocephala*

DATE   ☐ *seen*   ☐ *heard*

LOCATION

HABITAT

REMARKS

The White-crowned Pigeon, Audubon observed, "exhibits little of the pomposity of the common domestic species, in its amorous moments."

Red-billed Pigeon   *Columba flavirostris*

DATE   ☐ *seen*   ☐ *heard*

LOCATION

HABITAT

REMARKS

Band-tailed Pigeon *Columba fasciata*

DATE   ☐ *seen*   ☐ *heard*

LOCATION

HABITAT

REMARKS

Eurasian Collared-Dove *Streptopelia decaocto*

DATE   ☐ *seen*   ☐ *heard*

LOCATION

HABITAT

REMARKS

Ringed Turtle-Dove *Streptopelia risoria*

DATE   ☐ *seen*   ☐ *heard*

LOCATION

HABITAT

REMARKS

Spotted Dove *Streptopelia chinensis*

DATE   ☐ *seen*   ☐ *heard*

LOCATION

HABITAT

REMARKS

White-winged Dove *Zenaida asiatica*

DATE   ☐ *seen*   ☐ *heard*

LOCATION

HABITAT

REMARKS

Mourning Dove *Zenaida macroura*

DATE   ☐ *seen*   ☐ *heard*

LOCATION

HABITAT

REMARKS

Inca Dove *Columbina inca*

DATE   ☐ *seen*   ☐ *heard*

LOCATION

HABITAT

REMARKS

Common Ground-Dove *Columbina passerina*

DATE   ☐ *seen*   ☐ *heard*

LOCATION

HABITAT

REMARKS

The ground, Audubon noted, "is the usual resort" of the Common Ground-Dove: "There it runs with facility, keeping its tail considerably elevated, as if to save it from being soiled."

Passenger Pigeon ‡ (PLATE LXII)

White-tipped Dove	*Leptotila verreauxi*
DATE	☐ *seen* ☐ *heard*
LOCATION	
HABITAT	
REMARKS	

‡EXTINCT The last wild Passenger Pigeon was shot in Ohio in 1900. A captive bird survived until 1914, marking the extinction of a bird once so abundant it was believed to have outnumbered all other birds in the United States combined.

PARROTS	*Psittacidae*
Budgerigar	*Melopsittacus undulatus*
DATE	☐ *seen* ☐ *heard*
LOCATION	
HABITAT	
REMARKS	

Canary-winged Parakeet	*Brotogeris versicolurus*
DATE	☐ *seen* ☐ *heard*
LOCATION	
HABITAT	
REMARKS	

CUCKOOS	*Cuculidae*
Black-billed Cuckoo	*Coccyzus erythropthalmus*
DATE	☐ *seen* ☐ *heard*
LOCATION	
HABITAT	
REMARKS	

Yellow-billed Cuckoo   *Coccyzus americanus*

DATE   ☐ *seen*   ☐ *heard*

LOCATION

HABITAT

REMARKS

Mangrove Cuckoo   *Coccyzus minor*

DATE   ☐ *seen*   ☐ *heard*

LOCATION

HABITAT

REMARKS

Greater Roadrunner   *Geococcyx californianus*

DATE   ☐ *seen*   ☐ *heard*

LOCATION

HABITAT

REMARKS

Smooth-billed Ani   *Crotophaga ani*

DATE   ☐ *seen*   ☐ *heard*

LOCATION

HABITAT

REMARKS

Groove-billed Ani   *Crotophaga sulcirostris*

DATE   ☐ *seen*   ☐ *heard*

LOCATION

HABITAT

REMARKS

BARN OWLS   *Tytonidae*

Barn Owl   *Tyto alba*

DATE   ☐ *seen*   ☐ *heard*

LOCATION

HABITAT

REMARKS

TYPICAL OWLS   *Strigidae*

Flammulated Owl   *Otus flammeolus*

DATE   ☐ *seen*   ☐ *heard*

LOCATION

HABITAT

REMARKS

Eastern Screech-Owl   *Otus asio*

DATE   ☐ *seen*   ☐ *heard*

LOCATION

HABITAT

REMARKS

Audubon carried a young Eastern Screech-Owl in his coat pocket during a trip from Philadelphia to New York. "It remained generally quiet," he wrote, "fed from my hand, and never attempted to escape. I lost it at sea during my voyage to England in 1831."

Snowy Owl (PLATE CXXI)

Western Screech-Owl — *Otus kennicottii*

DATE ☐ *seen* ☐ *heard*

LOCATION

HABITAT

REMARKS

Whiskered Screech-Owl — *Otus trichopsis*

DATE ☐ *seen* ☐ *heard*

LOCATION

HABITAT

REMARKS

Great Horned Owl — *Bubo virginianus*

DATE ☐ *seen* ☐ *heard*

LOCATION

HABITAT

REMARKS

Snowy Owl — *Nyctea scandiaca*

DATE ☐ *seen* ☐ *heard*

LOCATION

HABITAT

REMARKS

Northern Hawk Owl   *Surnia ulula*

DATE   ☐ *seen*   ☐ *heard*

LOCATION

HABITAT

REMARKS

Northern Pygmy-Owl   *Glaucidium gnoma*

DATE   ☐ *seen*   ☐ *heard*

LOCATION

HABITAT

REMARKS

Ferruginous Pygmy-Owl   *Glaucidium brasilianum*

DATE   ☐ *seen*   ☐ *heard*

LOCATION

HABITAT

REMARKS

Elf Owl   *Micrathene whitneyi*

DATE   ☐ *seen*   ☐ *heard*

LOCATION

HABITAT

REMARKS

Burrowing Owl *Athene cunicularia*

DATE ☐ *seen* ☐ *heard*

LOCATION

HABITAT

REMARKS

Spotted Owl ‡ *Strix occidentalis*

DATE ☐ *seen* ☐ *heard*

LOCATION

HABITAT

REMARKS

‡THREATENED The northern subspecies of the Spotted Owl was added to the threatened list in summer 1990, triggering a bitter fight over old-growth logging in the Pacific Northwest. In fall 1991, biologists proposed adding the southwestern subspecies, too. The California population will likely follow.

Barred Owl *Strix varia*

DATE ☐ *seen* ☐ *heard*

LOCATION

HABITAT

REMARKS

Great Gray Owl *Strix nebulosa*

DATE ☐ *seen* ☐ *heard*

LOCATION

HABITAT

REMARKS

Long-eared Owl *Asio otus*

DATE _____ ☐ *seen* ☐ *heard*

LOCATION _____

HABITAT _____

REMARKS _____

_____

Short-eared Owl *Asio flammeus*

DATE _____ ☐ *seen* ☐ *heard*

LOCATION _____

HABITAT _____

REMARKS _____

_____

Boreal Owl *Aegolius funereus*

DATE _____ ☐ *seen* ☐ *heard*

LOCATION _____

HABITAT _____

REMARKS _____

_____

Northern Saw-whet Owl *Aegolius acadicus*

DATE _____ ☐ *seen* ☐ *heard*

LOCATION _____

HABITAT _____

REMARKS _____

_____

Great Gray Owl (Great Cinereous Owl, PLATE CCCLI)

Lesser Nighthawk   *Chordeiles acutipennis*

DATE   ☐ *seen*   ☐ *heard*

LOCATION

HABITAT

REMARKS

Common Nighthawk   *Chordeiles minor*

DATE   ☐ *seen*   ☐ *heard*

LOCATION

HABITAT

REMARKS

Antillean Nighthawk   *Chordeiles gundlachii*

DATE   ☐ *seen*   ☐ *heard*

LOCATION

HABITAT

REMARKS

Pauraque   *Nyctidromus albicollis*

DATE   ☐ *seen*   ☐ *heard*

LOCATION

HABITAT

REMARKS

Common Poorwill · *Phalaenoptilus nuttallii*

DATE _____ ☐ *seen* ☐ *heard*

LOCATION _____

HABITAT _____

REMARKS _____

_____

_____

Chuck-will's-widow · *Caprimulgus carolinensis*

DATE _____ ☐ *seen* ☐ *heard*

LOCATION _____

HABITAT _____

REMARKS _____

_____

_____

Buff-collared Nightjar · *Caprimulgus ridgwayi*

DATE _____ ☐ *seen* ☐ *heard*

LOCATION _____

HABITAT _____

REMARKS _____

_____

_____

Whip-poor-will · *Caprimulgus vociferus*

DATE _____ ☐ *seen* ☐ *heard*

LOCATION _____

HABITAT _____

REMARKS _____

_____

_____

The Common Poorwill was one of the last species Audubon discovered. He named it Nuttall's Whip-poor-will, after the naturalist Thomas Nuttall, who is still remembered in the bird's Latin name.

Black Swift   *Cypseloides niger*

DATE   ☐ *seen*   ☐ *heard*

LOCATION

HABITAT

REMARKS

"With judgment worth noting," Audubon commented on the Chimney Swift, "it has abandoned the hollows of trees and taken possession of the chimneys, which give forth no smoke in summer. Thus it has acquired its name."

Chimney Swift   *Chaetura pelagica*

DATE   ☐ *seen*   ☐ *heard*

LOCATION

HABITAT

REMARKS

Vaux's Swift   *Chaetura vauxi*

DATE   ☐ *seen*   ☐ *heard*

LOCATION

HABITAT

REMARKS

White-throated Swift   *Aeronautes saxatalis*

DATE   ☐ *seen*   ☐ *heard*

LOCATION

HABITAT

REMARKS

Broad-billed Hummingbird *Cynanthus latirostris*

DATE ☐ *seen* ☐ *heard*

LOCATION

HABITAT

REMARKS

White-eared Hummingbird *Hylocharis leucotis*

DATE ☐ *seen* ☐ *heard*

LOCATION

HABITAT

REMARKS

Berylline Hummingbird *Amazilia beryllina*

DATE ☐ *seen* ☐ *heard*

LOCATION

HABITAT

REMARKS

Buff-bellied Hummingbird *Amazilia yucatanensis*

DATE ☐ *seen* ☐ *heard*

LOCATION

HABITAT

REMARKS

Anna's Hummingbird (Columbian Humming Bird, PLATE CCCCXXV)

Rufous Hummingbird (Ruff-necked Humming-bird, PLATE CCCLXXIX)

Violet-crowned Hummingbird   *Amazilia violiceps*

DATE   □ *seen*   □ *heard*

LOCATION

HABITAT

REMARKS

Blue-throated Hummingbird   *Lampornis clemenciae*

DATE   □ *seen*   □ *heard*

LOCATION

HABITAT

REMARKS

Magnificent Hummingbird   *Eugenes fulgens*

DATE   □ *seen*   □ *heard*

LOCATION

HABITAT

REMARKS

Lucifer Hummingbird   *Calothorax lucifer*

DATE   □ *seen*   □ *heard*

LOCATION

HABITAT

REMARKS

Ruby-throated Hummingbird	*Archilochus colubris*

DATE ☐ *seen* ☐ *heard*

LOCATION

HABITAT

REMARKS

The Ruby-throated Hummingbird sent Audubon into dumb rapture: "I wish it were in my power to impart to you the delight I have felt while watching a pair of these most favorite little creatures displaying their feelings and love for each other."

Black-chinned Hummingbird	*Archilochus alexandri*

DATE ☐ *seen* ☐ *heard*

LOCATION

HABITAT

REMARKS

Anna's Hummingbird	*Calypte anna*

DATE ☐ *seen* ☐ *heard*

LOCATION

HABITAT

REMARKS

Costa's Hummingbird	*Calypte costae*

DATE ☐ *seen* ☐ *heard*

LOCATION

HABITAT

REMARKS

Calliope Hummingbird   *Stellula calliope*

DATE   ☐ *seen*   ☐ *heard*

LOCATION

HABITAT

REMARKS

Broad-tailed Hummingbird   *Selasphorus platycercus*

DATE   ☐ *seen*   ☐ *heard*

LOCATION

HABITAT

REMARKS

Rufous Hummingbird   *Selasphorus rufus*

DATE   ☐ *seen*   ☐ *heard*

LOCATION

HABITAT

REMARKS

Allen's Hummingbird   *Selasphorus sasin*

DATE   ☐ *seen*   ☐ *heard*

LOCATION

HABITAT

REMARKS

Elegant Trogon — *Trogon elegans*

DATE ☐ *seen* ☐ *heard*

LOCATION

HABITAT

REMARKS

KINGFISHERS *Alcedinidae*

Ringed Kingfisher — *Ceryle torquata*

DATE ☐ *seen* ☐ *heard*

LOCATION

HABITAT

REMARKS

Belted Kingfisher — *Ceryle alcyon*

DATE ☐ *seen* ☐ *heard*

LOCATION

HABITAT

REMARKS

Audubon believed that the Belted Kingfisher should be renamed, in part so that attention might be diverted away from the uppity females: ". . . although males, from time immemorial, have had supremacy, in this case the term *belted* is applicable only to the female."

Green Kingfisher — *Chloroceryle americana*

DATE ☐ *seen* ☐ *heard*

LOCATION

HABITAT

REMARKS

Lewis' Woodpecker   *Melanerpes lewis*

DATE   ☐ *seen*   ☐ *heard*

LOCATION

HABITAT

REMARKS

Red-headed Woodpecker   *Melanerpes erythrocephalus*

DATE   ☐ *seen*   ☐ *heard*

LOCATION

HABITAT

REMARKS

Acorn Woodpecker   *Melanerpes formicivorus*

DATE   ☐ *seen*   ☐ *heard*

LOCATION

HABITAT

REMARKS

Gila Woodpecker   *Melanerpes uropygialis*

DATE   ☐ *seen*   ☐ *heard*

LOCATION

HABITAT

REMARKS

Golden-fronted Woodpecker *Melanerpes aurifrons*

DATE ☐ *seen* ☐ *heard*

LOCATION

HABITAT

REMARKS

Red-bellied Woodpecker *Melanerpes carolinus*

DATE ☐ *seen* ☐ *heard*

LOCATION

HABITAT

REMARKS

Yellow-bellied Sapsucker *Sphyrapicus varius*

DATE ☐ *seen* ☐ *heard*

LOCATION

HABITAT

REMARKS

Red-naped Sapsucker *Sphyrapicus nuchalis*

DATE ☐ *seen* ☐ *heard*

LOCATION

HABITAT

REMARKS

Red-breasted Sapsucker *Sphyrapicus ruber*

DATE ☐ *seen* ☐ *heard*

LOCATION

HABITAT

REMARKS

Williamson's Sapsucker *Sphyrapicus thyroideus*

DATE ☐ *seen* ☐ *heard*

LOCATION

HABITAT

REMARKS

Ladder-backed Woodpecker *Picoides scalaris*

DATE ☐ *seen* ☐ *heard*

LOCATION

HABITAT

REMARKS

Nuttall's Woodpecker *Picoides nuttallii*

DATE ☐ *seen* ☐ *heard*

LOCATION

HABITAT

REMARKS

Ivory-billed Woodpecker‡ (PLATE LXVI)

Downy Woodpecker   *Picoides pubescens*

DATE   ☐ *seen*   ☐ *heard*

LOCATION

HABITAT

REMARKS

Hairy Woodpecker   *Picoides villosus*

DATE   ☐ *seen*   ☐ *heard*

LOCATION

HABITAT

REMARKS

Strickland's Woodpecker   *Picoides stricklandi*

DATE   ☐ *seen*   ☐ *heard*

LOCATION

HABITAT

REMARKS

‡ENDANGERED Sometimes called the Spotted Owl of the Southeastern pine forest, the Red-cockaded Woodpecker continues to decline because its habitat requirements are at odds with modern logging practices.

Red-cockaded Woodpecker‡   *Picoides borealis*

DATE   ☐ *seen*   ☐ *heard*

LOCATION

HABITAT

REMARKS

White-headed Woodpecker *Picoides albolarvatus*

DATE ☐ *seen* ☐ *heard*

LOCATION

HABITAT

REMARKS

Three-toed Woodpecker *Picoides tridactylus*

DATE ☐ *seen* ☐ *heard*

LOCATION

HABITAT

REMARKS

Black-backed Woodpecker *Picoides arcticus*

DATE ☐ *seen* ☐ *heard*

LOCATION

HABITAT

REMARKS

Northern Flicker *Colaptes auratus*

DATE ☐ *seen* ☐ *heard*

LOCATION

HABITAT

REMARKS

Audubon found the Northern Flicker – or the Golden-winged Woodpecker, as he knew it – for sale as meat in the markets of New Orleans.

Pileated Woodpecker   *Dryocopus pileatus*

DATE _____   ☐ *seen*   ☐ *heard*

LOCATION _____

HABITAT _____

REMARKS _____

_____

‡ENDANGERED A former inhabitant of tangled Southern swamps, the Ivory-billed Woodpecker, shot and logged to oblivion, will likely soon be declared officially extinct. Audubon found the bird in "those deep morasses overshadowed by millions of gigantic, dark, moss-covered cypresses which seem to admonish intruding man to pause and reflect on the many difficulties ahead."

Ivory-billed Woodpecker ‡   *Campephilus principalis*

DATE _____   ☐ *seen*   ☐ *heard*

LOCATION _____

HABITAT _____

REMARKS _____

_____

PASSERIFORMES

Northern Beardless-Tyrannulet   *Camptostoma imberbe*

DATE _____   ☐ *seen*   ☐ *heard*

LOCATION _____

HABITAT _____

REMARKS _____

_____

Olive-sided Flycatcher   *Contopus borealis*

DATE _____   ☐ *seen*   ☐ *heard*

LOCATION _____

HABITAT _____

REMARKS _____

_____

Greater Pewee *Contopus pertinax*

DATE ☐ *seen* ☐ *heard*

LOCATION

HABITAT

REMARKS

Western Wood-Pewee *Contopus sordidulus*

DATE ☐ *seen* ☐ *heard*

LOCATION

HABITAT

REMARKS

Eastern Wood-Pewee *Contopus virens*

DATE ☐ *seen* ☐ *heard*

LOCATION

HABITAT

REMARKS

Audubon compared the call of the Eastern Wood-Pewee to "the last sighs of a despondent lover."

Yellow-bellied Flycatcher *Empidonax flaviventris*

DATE ☐ *seen* ☐ *heard*

LOCATION

HABITAT

REMARKS

Acadian Flycatcher   *Empidonax virescens*

DATE   ☐ *seen*   ☐ *heard*

LOCATION

HABITAT

REMARKS

Alder Flycatcher   *Empidonax alnorum*

DATE   ☐ *seen*   ☐ *heard*

LOCATION

HABITAT

REMARKS

Willow Flycatcher   *Empidonax traillii*

DATE   ☐ *seen*   ☐ *heard*

LOCATION

HABITAT

REMARKS

Least Flycatcher   *Empidonax minimus*

DATE   ☐ *seen*   ☐ *heard*

LOCATION

HABITAT

REMARKS

Hammond's Flycatcher *Empidonax hammondii*

DATE ☐ *seen* ☐ *heard*

LOCATION

HABITAT

REMARKS

Dusky Flycatcher *Empidonax oberholseri*

DATE ☐ *seen* ☐ *heard*

LOCATION

HABITAT

REMARKS

Gray Flycatcher *Empidonax wrightii*

DATE ☐ *seen* ☐ *heard*

LOCATION

HABITAT

REMARKS

Pacific-slope Flycatcher *Empidonax difficilis*

DATE ☐ *seen* ☐ *heard*

LOCATION

HABITAT

REMARKS

Cordilleran Flycatcher   *Empidonax occidentalis*

DATE   ☐ *seen*   ☐ *heard*

LOCATION

HABITAT

REMARKS

Buff-breasted Flycatcher   *Empidonax fulvifrons*

DATE   ☐ *seen*   ☐ *heard*

LOCATION

HABITAT

REMARKS

Black Phoebe   *Sayornis nigricans*

DATE   ☐ *seen*   ☐ *heard*

LOCATION

HABITAT

REMARKS

Eastern Phoebe   *Sayornis phoebe*

DATE   ☐ *seen*   ☐ *heard*

LOCATION

HABITAT

REMARKS

Audubon had a sentimental attachment to Eastern Phoebes. They recalled to him "the youthful days of an American woodsman." After he sold Mill Grove in Pennsylvania, he was chagrined to see that the cave where phoebes nested was destroyed for the construction of a new dam across Perkiomen Creek.

Say's Phoebe — *Sayornis saya*

DATE ☐ *seen* ☐ *heard*

LOCATION

HABITAT

REMARKS

Vermilion Flycatcher — *Pyrocephalus rubinus*

DATE ☐ *seen* ☐ *heard*

LOCATION

HABITAT

REMARKS

Dusky-capped Flycatcher — *Myiarchus tuberculifer*

DATE ☐ *seen* ☐ *heard*

LOCATION

HABITAT

REMARKS

Ash-throated Flycatcher — *Myiarchus cinerascens*

DATE ☐ *seen* ☐ *heard*

LOCATION

HABITAT

REMARKS

Great Crested Flycatcher   *Myiarchus crinitus*

DATE   ☐ *seen*   ☐ *heard*

LOCATION

HABITAT

REMARKS

Brown-crested Flycatcher   *Myiarchus tyrannulus*

DATE   ☐ *seen*   ☐ *heard*

LOCATION

HABITAT

REMARKS

Great Kiskadee   *Pitangus sulphuratus*

DATE   ☐ *seen*   ☐ *heard*

LOCATION

HABITAT

REMARKS

Sulphur-bellied Flycatcher   *Myiodynastes luteiventris*

DATE   ☐ *seen*   ☐ *heard*

LOCATION

HABITAT

REMARKS

Tropical Kingbird — *Tyrannus melancholicus*

DATE ☐ *seen* ☐ *heard*

LOCATION

HABITAT

REMARKS

Couch's Kingbird — *Tyrannus couchii*

DATE ☐ *seen* ☐ *heard*

LOCATION

HABITAT

REMARKS

Cassin's Kingbird — *Tyrannus vociferans*

DATE ☐ *seen* ☐ *heard*

LOCATION

HABITAT

REMARKS

Thick-billed Kingbird — *Tyrannus crassirostris*

DATE ☐ *seen* ☐ *heard*

LOCATION

HABITAT

REMARKS

Western Kingbird   *Tyrannus verticalis*

DATE   ☐ *seen*   ☐ *heard*

LOCATION

HABITAT

REMARKS

Eastern Kingbird   *Tyrannus tyrannus*

DATE   ☐ *seen*   ☐ *heard*

LOCATION

HABITAT

REMARKS

In the Florida Keys, Audubon admired the Gray Kingbird and experienced bliss: "Reader, such are the moments, amid days of toil and discomfort, that compensate for every privation."

Gray Kingbird   *Tyrannus dominicensis*

DATE   ☐ *seen*   ☐ *heard*

LOCATION

HABITAT

REMARKS

Scissor-tailed Flycatcher   *Tyrannus forficatus*

DATE   ☐ *seen*   ☐ *heard*

LOCATION

HABITAT

REMARKS

Fork-tailed Flycatcher *Tyrannus savana*

DATE ☐ *seen* ☐ *heard*

LOCATION

HABITAT

REMARKS

Rose-throated Becard *Pachyramphus aglaiae*

DATE ☐ *seen* ☐ *heard*

LOCATION

HABITAT

REMARKS

LARKS *Alaudidae*

Eurasian Skylark *Alauda arvensis*

DATE ☐ *seen* ☐ *heard*

LOCATION

HABITAT

REMARKS

Horned Lark *Eremophila alpestris*

DATE ☐ *seen* ☐ *heard*

LOCATION

HABITAT

REMARKS

The California subspecies of the Horned Lark is a candidate for review under the Endangered Species Act.

Audubon admired how the
Purple Martin drinks while fly-
ing over a lake or river: "As it
comes in contact with the
water it dips in the hind part of
the body with a sudden
motion, then rises and shakes
like a water spaniel."

Purple Martin   *Progne subis*

DATE   ☐ *seen*   ☐ *heard*

LOCATION

HABITAT

REMARKS

Tree Swallow   *Tachycineta bicolor*

DATE   ☐ *seen*   ☐ *heard*

LOCATION

HABITAT

REMARKS

Violet-green Swallow   *Tachycineta thalassina*

DATE   ☐ *seen*   ☐ *heard*

LOCATION

HABITAT

REMARKS

Northern Rough-winged Swallow   *Stelgidopteryx serripennis*

DATE   ☐ *seen*   ☐ *heard*

LOCATION

HABITAT

REMARKS

Bank Swallow   *Riparia riparia*

DATE   ☐ *seen*   ☐ *heard*

LOCATION

HABITAT

REMARKS

Cliff Swallow   *Hirundo pyrrhonota*

DATE   ☐ *seen*   ☐ *heard*

LOCATION

HABITAT

REMARKS

Cave Swallow   *Hirundo fulva*

DATE   ☐ *seen*   ☐ *heard*

LOCATION

HABITAT

REMARKS

Barn Swallow   *Hirundo rustica*

DATE   ☐ *seen*   ☐ *heard*

LOCATION

HABITAT

REMARKS

"In *The Birds of America* I have shown a pair of Barn Swallows in their most perfect spring plumage, with a nest from the rafter of a barn in New Jersey, in which there was at least a score of them."

Barn Swallow (PLATE CLXXIII)

Gray Jay — *Perisoreus canadensis*

DATE   ☐ *seen*   ☐ *heard*

LOCATION

HABITAT

REMARKS

Steller's Jay — *Cyanocitta stelleri*

DATE   ☐ *seen*   ☐ *heard*

LOCATION

HABITAT

REMARKS

Blue Jay — *Cyanocitta cristata*

DATE   ☐ *seen*   ☐ *heard*

LOCATION

HABITAT

REMARKS

Green Jay — *Cyanocorax yncas*

DATE   ☐ *seen*   ☐ *heard*

LOCATION

HABITAT

REMARKS

Brown Jay   *Cyanocorax morio*

DATE   ☐ *seen*   ☐ *heard*

LOCATION

HABITAT

REMARKS

‡ENDANGERED Although the Scrub Jay is found over a wide area in the West, the Florida population, uncommon even in Audubon's day, is now endangered. Its sandy, dry habitat has been a favorite of real-estate developers in this generally swampy state.

Scrub Jay ‡   *Aphelocoma coerulescens*

DATE   ☐ *seen*   ☐ *heard*

LOCATION

HABITAT

REMARKS

Gray-breasted Jay   *Aphelocoma ultramarina*

DATE   ☐ *seen*   ☐ *heard*

LOCATION

HABITAT

REMARKS

Pinyon Jay   *Gymnorhinus cyanocephalus*

DATE   ☐ *seen*   ☐ *heard*

LOCATION

HABITAT

REMARKS

Clark's Nutcracker *Nucifraga columbiana*

DATE ☐ *seen* ☐ *heard*

LOCATION

HABITAT

REMARKS

Black-billed Magpie *Pica pica*

DATE ☐ *seen* ☐ *heard*

LOCATION

HABITAT

REMARKS

Yellow-billed Magpie *Pica nuttalli*

DATE ☐ *seen* ☐ *heard*

LOCATION

HABITAT

REMARKS

American Crow *Corvus brachyrhynchos*

DATE ☐ *seen* ☐ *heard*

LOCATION

HABITAT

REMARKS

"Wherever within the Union the laws encourage the destruction of this species," Audubon wrote of the American Crow, "it is shot in great numbers for the sake of the premium offered for each crow's head. You will perhaps be surprised, reader, when I tell you that in one single State, in the course of a season, 40,000 were shot . . . ."

Northwestern Crow   *Corvus caurinus*

DATE   ☐ *seen*   ☐ *heard*

LOCATION

HABITAT

REMARKS

Mexican Crow   *Corvus imparatus*

DATE `   ☐ *seen*   ☐ *heard*

LOCATION

HABITAT

REMARKS

Fish Crow   *Corvus ossifragus*

DATE   ☐ *seen*   ☐ *heard*

LOCATION

HABITAT

REMARKS

Chihuahuan Raven   *Corvus cryptoleucus*

DATE   ☐ *seen*   ☐ *heard*

LOCATION

HABITAT

REMARKS

Common Raven — *Corvus corax*

DATE ☐ *seen* ☐ *heard*

LOCATION

HABITAT

REMARKS

TITMICE — *Paridae*

Black-capped Chickadee — *Parus atricapillus*

DATE ☐ *seen* ☐ *heard*

LOCATION

HABITAT

REMARKS

Carolina Chickadee — *Parus carolinensis*

DATE ☐ *seen* ☐ *heard*

LOCATION

HABITAT

REMARKS

Mexican Chickadee — *Parus sclateri*

DATE ☐ *seen* ☐ *heard*

LOCATION

HABITAT

REMARKS

Mountain Chickadee   *Parus gambeli*

DATE   ☐ *seen*   ☐ *heard*

LOCATION

HABITAT

REMARKS

Siberian Tit   *Parus cinctus*

DATE   ☐ *seen*   ☐ *heard*

LOCATION

HABITAT

REMARKS

Audubon found the Boreal Chickadee in Labrador: "In crossing what is here called a wood, we found a nest of *Parus hudsonicus* containing four young, able to fly; we procured the parents also, and I shall have the pleasure of drawing them tomorrow; this bird has never been figured that I know."

Boreal Chickadee   *Parus hudsonicus*

DATE   ☐ *seen*   ☐ *heard*

LOCATION

HABITAT

REMARKS

Chestnut-backed Chickadee   *Parus rufescens*

DATE   ☐ *seen*   ☐ *heard*

LOCATION

HABITAT

REMARKS

Bridled Titmouse — *Parus wollweberi*

DATE ☐ *seen* ☐ *heard*

LOCATION

HABITAT

REMARKS

Plain Titmouse — *Parus inornatus*

DATE ☐ *seen* ☐ *heard*

LOCATION

HABITAT

REMARKS

Tufted Titmouse — *Parus bicolor*

DATE ☐ *seen* ☐ *heard*

LOCATION

HABITAT

REMARKS

VERDINS — *Remizidae*

Verdin — *Auriparus flaviceps*

DATE ☐ *seen* ☐ *heard*

LOCATION

HABITAT

REMARKS

Tufted Titmouse (Crested Titmouse, PLATE XXXIX)

Brown Creeper & Pigmy Nuthatch
(Brown Creeper & Californian Nuthatch, PLATE CCCCXV)

Bushtit   Psaltriparus minimus

DATE   ☐ *seen*   ☐ *heard*

LOCATION

HABITAT

REMARKS

NUTHATCHES   *Sittidae*

Red-breasted Nuthatch   *Sitta canadensis*

DATE   ☐ *seen*   ☐ *heard*

LOCATION

HABITAT

REMARKS

White-breasted Nuthatch   *Sitta carolinensis*

DATE   ☐ *seen*   ☐ *heard*

LOCATION

HABITAT

REMARKS

Pygmy Nuthatch   *Sitta pygmaea*

DATE   ☐ *seen*   ☐ *heard*

LOCATION

HABITAT

REMARKS

Brown-headed Nuthatch — *Sitta pusilla*

DATE ☐ *seen* ☐ *heard*

LOCATION

HABITAT

REMARKS

CREEPERS *Certhiidae*

Brown Creeper — *Certhia americana*

DATE ☐ *seen* ☐ *heard*

LOCATION

HABITAT

REMARKS

BULBULS *Pycnonotidae*

Red-whiskered Bulbul — *Pycnonotus jocosus*

DATE ☐ *seen* ☐ *heard*

LOCATION

HABITAT

REMARKS

WRENS *Troglodytidae*

Cactus Wren — *Campylorhynchus brunneicapillus*

DATE ☐ *seen* ☐ *heard*

LOCATION

HABITAT

REMARKS

Bewick's Wren (Bewick's Long-tailed Wren, PLATE XVIII)

Rock Wren	*Salpinctes obsoletus*
DATE	☐ *seen* ☐ *heard*
LOCATION	
HABITAT	
REMARKS	

Canyon Wren	*Catherpes mexicanus*
DATE	☐ *seen* ☐ *heard*
LOCATION	
HABITAT	
REMARKS	

Carolina Wren	*Thryothorus ludovicianus*
DATE	☐ *seen* ☐ *heard*
LOCATION	
HABITAT	
REMARKS	

Bewick's Wren	*Thryomanes bewickii*
DATE	☐ *seen* ☐ *heard*
LOCATION	
HABITAT	
REMARKS	

The Appalachian subspecies of the Bewick's Wren is declining and may be a candidate for threatened or endangered status. Audubon named the bird after his friend Thomas Bewick, the author and illustrator of *A History of British Birds*.

House Wren   *Troglodytes aedon*

DATE   ☐ *seen*   ☐ *heard*

LOCATION

HABITAT

REMARKS

"Dull indeed must be the ear that thrills not on hearing it," wrote Audubon about the bright and intricate song of the Winter Wren.

Winter Wren   *Troglodytes troglodytes*

DATE   ☐ *seen*   ☐ *heard*

LOCATION

HABITAT

REMARKS

Sedge Wren   *Cistothorus platensis*

DATE   ☐ *seen*   ☐ *heard*

LOCATION

HABITAT

REMARKS

Marsh Wren   *Cistothorus palustris*

DATE   ☐ *seen*   ☐ *heard*

LOCATION

HABITAT

REMARKS

American Dipper — *Cinclus mexicanus*

DATE ☐ *seen* ☐ *heard*

LOCATION

HABITAT

REMARKS

OLD WORLD WARBLERS — *Muscicapidae*

Arctic Warbler — *Phylloscopus borealis*

DATE ☐ *seen* ☐ *heard*

LOCATION

HABITAT

REMARKS

Golden-crowned Kinglet — *Regulus satrapa*

DATE ☐ *seen* ☐ *heard*

LOCATION

HABITAT

REMARKS

Ruby-crowned Kinglet — *Regulus calendula*

DATE ☐ *seen* ☐ *heard*

LOCATION

HABITAT

REMARKS

Eastern Bluebird (Blue-bird, PLATE CXIII)

Blue-gray Gnatcatcher　　*Polioptila caerulea*

DATE ☐ *seen* ☐ *heard*

LOCATION

HABITAT

REMARKS

California Gnatcatcher　　*Polioptila californica*

DATE ☐ *seen* ☐ *heard*

LOCATION

HABITAT

REMARKS

Although not declared a species until 1989, the California Gnatcatcher became a candidate for the Endangered Species List two years later. Urban encroachment has destroyed much of the sagegrush habitat of the coastal southern California population.

Black-tailed Gnatcatcher　　*Polioptila melanura*

DATE ☐ *seen* ☐ *heard*

LOCATION

HABITAT

REMARKS

Black-capped Gnatcatcher　　*Polioptila nigriceps*

DATE ☐ *seen* ☐ *heard*

LOCATION

HABITAT

REMARKS

Siberian Rubythroat   *Luscinia calliope*

DATE   ☐ *seen*   ☐ *heard*

LOCATION

HABITAT

REMARKS

Bluethroat   *Luscinia svecica*

DATE   ☐ *seen*   ☐ *heard*

LOCATION

HABITAT

REMARKS

Northern Wheatear   *Oenanthe oenanthe*

DATE   ☐ *seen*   ☐ *heard*

LOCATION

HABITAT

REMARKS

Eastern Bluebird   *Sialia sialis*

DATE   ☐ *seen*   ☐ *heard*

LOCATION

HABITAT

REMARKS

Western Bluebird   *Sialia mexicana*

DATE   ☐ *seen*   ☐ *heard*

LOCATION

HABITAT

REMARKS

Mountain Bluebird   *Sialia currucoides*

DATE   ☐ *seen*   ☐ *heard*

LOCATION

HABITAT

REMARKS

Townsend's Solitaire   *Myadestes townsendi*

DATE   ☐ *seen*   ☐ *heard*

LOCATION

HABITAT

REMARKS

Veery   *Catharus fuscescens*

DATE   ☐ *seen*   ☐ *heard*

LOCATION

HABITAT

REMARKS

Gray-cheeked Thrush   *Catharus minimus*

DATE   ☐ *seen*   ☐ *heard*

LOCATION

HABITAT

REMARKS

Swainson's Thrush   *Catharus ustulatus*

DATE   ☐ *seen*   ☐ *heard*

LOCATION

HABITAT

REMARKS

Hermit Thrush   *Catharus guttatus*

DATE   ☐ *seen*   ☐ *heard*

LOCATION

HABITAT

REMARKS

Audubon: "The Wood Thrush is my greatest favorite of our feathered tribes. To it I owe much. Often when I have listened to its wild notes in the forest, it has revived my drooping spirits."

Wood Thrush   *Hylocichla mustelina*

DATE   ☐ *seen*   ☐ *heard*

LOCATION

HABITAT

REMARKS

Eyebrowed Thrush — *Turdus obscurus*

DATE ☐ *seen* ☐ *heard*

LOCATION

HABITAT

REMARKS

Clay-colored Robin — *Turdus grayi*

DATE ☐ *seen* ☐ *heard*

LOCATION

HABITAT

REMARKS

Rufous-backed Robin — *Turdus rufopalliatus*

DATE ☐ *seen* ☐ *heard*

LOCATION

HABITAT

REMARKS

American Robin — *Turdus migratorius*

DATE ☐ *seen* ☐ *heard*

LOCATION

HABITAT

REMARKS

THRUSHES   *Muscicapidae*

Varied Thrush   *Ixoreus naevius*

DATE   ☐ *seen*   ☐ *heard*

LOCATION

HABITAT

REMARKS

Wrentit   *Chamaea fasciata*

DATE   ☐ *seen*   ☐ *heard*

LOCATION

HABITAT

REMARKS

MOCKINGBIRDS & THRASHERS   *Mimidae*

Gray Catbird   *Dumetella carolinensis*

DATE   ☐ *seen*   ☐ *heard*

LOCATION

HABITAT

REMARKS

"The Mocking Birds are so Gentle that I followed one along a fence this morning for nearly one Mile," Audubon wrote in his journal for January 4, 1821.

Northern Mockingbird   *Mimus polyglottos*

DATE   ☐ *seen*   ☐ *heard*

LOCATION

HABITAT

REMARKS

Sage Thrasher   *Oreoscoptes montanus*

DATE   ☐ *seen*   ☐ *heard*

LOCATION

HABITAT

REMARKS

Brown Thrasher   *Toxostoma rufum*

DATE   ☐ *seen*   ☐ *heard*

LOCATION

HABITAT

REMARKS

Of the Brown Thrasher, Audubon observed: "The Brown Thrush is the strongest of its genus in the United States. . . . It will chase a dog or cat and tease a raccoon or fox. It will follow and defy the Cooper's Hawk and the Goshawk. Few snakes come off the victor when they attack its nest."

Long-billed Thrasher   *Toxostoma longirostre*

DATE   ☐ *seen*   ☐ *heard*

LOCATION

HABITAT

REMARKS

Bendire's Thrasher   *Toxostoma bendirei*

DATE   ☐ *seen*   ☐ *heard*

LOCATION

HABITAT

REMARKS

Curve-billed Thrasher   *Toxostoma curvirostre*

DATE   ☐ *seen*   ☐ *heard*

LOCATION

HABITAT

REMARKS

California Thrasher   *Toxostoma redivivum*

DATE   ☐ *seen*   ☐ *heard*

LOCATION

HABITAT

REMARKS

Crissal Thrasher   *Toxostoma crissale*

DATE   ☐ *seen*   ☐ *heard*

LOCATION

HABITAT

REMARKS

Le Conte's Thrasher   *Toxostoma lecontei*

DATE   ☐ *seen*   ☐ *heard*

LOCATION

HABITAT

REMARKS

Yellow Wagtail — *Motacilla flava*

DATE ☐ *seen* ☐ *heard*

LOCATION

HABITAT

REMARKS

White Wagtail — *Motacilla alba*

DATE ☐ *seen* ☐ *heard*

LOCATION

HABITAT

REMARKS

Black-backed Wagtail — *Motacilla lugens*

DATE ☐ *seen* ☐ *heard*

LOCATION

HABITAT

REMARKS

Olive Tree-Pipit — *Anthus hodgsoni*

DATE ☐ *seen* ☐ *heard*

LOCATION

HABITAT

REMARKS

Red-throated Pipit   *Anthus cervinus*

DATE   ☐ *seen*   ☐ *heard*

LOCATION

HABITAT

REMARKS

American Pipit   *Anthus rubescens*

DATE   ☐ *seen*   ☐ *heard*

LOCATION

HABITAT

REMARKS

Sprague's Pipit   *Anthus spragueii*

DATE   ☐ *seen*   ☐ *heard*

LOCATION

HABITAT

REMARKS

WAXWINGS   *Bombycillidae*

Bohemian Waxwing   *Bombycilla garrulus*

DATE   ☐ *seen*   ☐ *heard*

LOCATION

HABITAT

REMARKS

Cedar Waxwing (Cedar Bird, PLATE XLIII)

WAXWINGS   *Bombycillidae*

Cedar Waxwing   *Bombycilla cedrorum*

DATE   ☐ *seen*   ☐ *heard*

LOCATION

HABITAT

REMARKS

SILKY-FLYCATCHERS   *Ptilogonatidae*

Phainopepla   *Phainopepla nitens*

DATE   ☐ *seen*   ☐ *heard*

LOCATION

HABITAT

REMARKS

SHRIKES   *Laniidae*

Northern Shrike   *Lanius excubitor*

DATE   ☐ *seen*   ☐ *heard*

LOCATION

HABITAT

REMARKS

‡ENDANGERED The Logger-head Shrike is probably declining generally, but one subspecies, found on California's uninhabited San Clemente Island, is endangered, due to habitat destruction by feral goats.

Loggerhead Shrike‡   *Lanius ludovicianus*

DATE   ☐ *seen*   ☐ *heard*

LOCATION

HABITAT

REMARKS

European Starling — *Sturnus vulgaris*

DATE   □ *seen*   □ *heard*

LOCATION

HABITAT

REMARKS

Crested Myna — *Acridotheres cristatellus*

DATE   □ *seen*   □ *heard*

LOCATION

HABITAT

REMARKS

| VIREOS | *Vireonidae* |

White-eyed Vireo — *Vireo griseus*

DATE   □ *seen*   □ *heard*

LOCATION

HABITAT

REMARKS

Bell's Vireo ‡ — *Vireo bellii*

DATE   □ *seen*   □ *heard*

LOCATION

HABITAT

REMARKS

‡ENDANGERED Usually found near water, the Bell's Vireo is believed to be declining along with its riparian habitat. The Least Bell's Vireo, a California subspecies, is endangered.

Solitary Vireo (Solitary Flycatcher or Vireo, PLATE XXVIII)

Black-capped Vireo‡   *Vireo atricapillus*

DATE   ☐ *seen*   ☐ *heard*

LOCATION

HABITAT

REMARKS

Gray Vireo   *Vireo vicinior*

DATE   ☐ *seen*   ☐ *heard*

LOCATION

HABITAT

REMARKS

Solitary Vireo   *Vireo solitarius*

DATE   ☐ *seen*   ☐ *heard*

LOCATION

HABITAT

REMARKS

Yellow-throated Vireo   *Vireo flavifrons*

DATE   ☐ *seen*   ☐ *heard*

LOCATION

HABITAT

REMARKS

‡ENDANGERED Uncommon for many years, the Black-capped Vireo was added to the Endangered Species List in 1987. Fragmentation of its Texas-hill-country habitat has made it particularly vulnerable to parasitism from Brown-headed Cowbirds.

Hutton's Vireo — *Vireo huttoni*

DATE ☐ *seen* ☐ *heard*

LOCATION

HABITAT

REMARKS

Warbling Vireo — *Vireo gilvus*

DATE ☐ *seen* ☐ *heard*

LOCATION

HABITAT

REMARKS

Philadelphia Vireo — *Vireo philadelphicus*

DATE ☐ *seen* ☐ *heard*

LOCATION

HABITAT

REMARKS

Red-eyed Vireo — *Vireo olivaceus*

DATE ☐ *seen* ☐ *heard*

LOCATION

HABITAT

REMARKS

Yellow-green Vireo — Vireo flavoviridis

☐ *seen* ☐ *heard*

DATE

LOCATION

HABITAT

REMARKS

Black-whiskered Vireo — *Vireo altiloquus*

☐ *seen* ☐ *heard*

DATE

LOCATION

HABITAT

REMARKS

WOOD WARBLERS — *Emberizidae, subfamily Parulinae*

Bachman's Warbler ‡ — *Vermivora bachmanii*

☐ *seen* ☐ *heard*

DATE

LOCATION

HABITAT

REMARKS

‡ENDANGERED Named after Audubon's close friend, Dr. John Bachman, a South Carolina minister, the Bachman's Warbler is probably extinct in the U.S. Over the last decade, there have been only a few reliable sightings, all in Cuba.

Blue-winged Warbler — *Vermivora pinus*

☐ *seen* ☐ *heard*

DATE

LOCATION

HABITAT

REMARKS

Golden-winged Warbler   *Vermivora chrysoptera*

DATE   ☐ *seen*   ☐ *heard*

LOCATION

HABITAT

REMARKS

Tennessee Warbler   *Vermivora peregrina*

DATE   ☐ *seen*   ☐ *heard*

LOCATION

HABITAT

REMARKS

Orange-crowned Warbler   *Vermivora celata*

DATE   ☐ *seen*   ☐ *heard*

LOCATION

HABITAT

REMARKS

Nashville Warbler   *Vermivora ruficapilla*

DATE   ☐ *seen*   ☐ *heard*

LOCATION

HABITAT

REMARKS

Chestnut-sided Warbler (PLATE LIX)

Virginia's Warbler   *Vermivora virginiae*

DATE   ☐ *seen*   ☐ *heard*

LOCATION

HABITAT

REMARKS

Colima Warbler   *Vermivora crissalis*

DATE   ☐ *seen*   ☐ *heard*

LOCATION

HABITAT

REMARKS

Lucy's Warbler   *Vermivora luciae*

DATE   ☐ *seen*   ☐ *heard*

LOCATION

HABITAT

REMARKS

Northern Parula   *Parula americana*

DATE   ☐ *seen*   ☐ *heard*

LOCATION

HABITAT

REMARKS

Tropical Parula	*Parula pitiayumi*
DATE	☐ *seen* ☐ *heard*
LOCATION	
HABITAT	
REMARKS	

The Texas population of the Tropical Parula is very small. It is a candidate for review under the Endangered Species Act.

Yellow Warbler	*Dendroica petechia*
DATE	☐ *seen* ☐ *heard*
LOCATION	
HABITAT	
REMARKS	

Chestnut-sided Warbler	*Dendroica pensylvanica*
DATE	☐ *seen* ☐ *heard*
LOCATION	
HABITAT	
REMARKS	

Magnolia Warbler	*Dendroica magnolia*
DATE	☐ *seen* ☐ *heard*
LOCATION	
HABITAT	
REMARKS	

Black-throated Blue Warbler (PLATE CLV)

Cape May Warbler *Dendroica tigrina*

DATE ☐ *seen* ☐ *heard*

LOCATION

HABITAT

REMARKS

Black-throated Blue Warbler *Dendroica caerulescens*

DATE ☐ *seen* ☐ *heard*

LOCATION

HABITAT

REMARKS

Fortunately, all the original paintings for *The Birds of America* have survived except two, which have been lost. One of these two was the model for plate CLV, the Black-throated Blue Warbler.

Yellow-rumped Warbler *Dendroica coronata*

DATE ☐ *seen* ☐ *heard*

LOCATION

HABITAT

REMARKS

Black-throated Gray Warbler *Dendroica nigrescens*

DATE ☐ *seen* ☐ *heard*

LOCATION

HABITAT

REMARKS

Townsend's Warbler   *Dendroica townsendi*

DATE   ☐ *seen*   ☐ *heard*

LOCATION

HABITAT

REMARKS

Hermit Warbler   *Dendroica occidentalis*

DATE   ☐ *seen*   ☐ *heard*

LOCATION

HABITAT

REMARKS

Black-throated Green Warbler   *Dendroica virens*

DATE   ☐ *seen*   ☐ *heard*

LOCATION

HABITAT

REMARKS

‡ENDANGERED Urbanization in central Texas has reduced the mature Ashe juniper and oak woodlands the Golden-cheeked Warbler needs to survive. It was listed as endangered in 1990.

Golden-cheeked Warbler‡   *Dendroica chrysoparia*

DATE   ☐ *seen*   ☐ *heard*

LOCATION

HABITAT

REMARKS

Blackburnian Warbler   *Dendroica fusca*

DATE   ☐ *seen*   ☐ *heard*

LOCATION

HABITAT

REMARKS

Yellow-throated Warbler   *Dendroica dominica*

DATE   ☐ *seen*   ☐ *heard*

LOCATION

HABITAT

REMARKS

Grace's Warbler   *Dendroica graciae*

DATE   ☐ *seen*   ☐ *heard*

LOCATION

HABITAT

REMARKS

Pine Warbler   *Dendroica pinus*

DATE   ☐ *seen*   ☐ *heard*

LOCATION

HABITAT

REMARKS

Yellow-throated Warbler (Yellow Throat Warbler, PLATE LXXXV)

Palm Warbler (Yellow Red-poll Warbler, PLATE CXLV)

‡ENDANGERED Found almost exclusively in lower Michigan, the Kirtland's Warbler has long been endangered. Recent bird counts indicate that it may be slowly increasing in numbers, thanks to careful habitat management.

Kirtland's Warbler‡   *Dendroica kirtlandii*

DATE   ☐ *seen*   ☐ *heard*

LOCATION

HABITAT

REMARKS

Prairie Warbler   *Dendroica discolor*

DATE   ☐ *seen*   ☐ *heard*

LOCATION

HABITAT

REMARKS

Palm Warbler   *Dendroica palmarum*

DATE   ☐ *seen*   ☐ *heard*

LOCATION

HABITAT

REMARKS

Bay-breasted Warbler   *Dendroica castanea*

DATE   ☐ *seen*   ☐ *heard*

LOCATION

HABITAT

REMARKS

Blackpoll Warbler   *Dendroica striata*

DATE   ☐ *seen*   ☐ *heard*

LOCATION

HABITAT

REMARKS

Cerulean Warbler   *Dendroica cerulea*

DATE   ☐ *seen*   ☐ *heard*

LOCATION

HABITAT

REMARKS

Uncommon, the Cerulean Warbler is a candidate for review for possible endangered status under the Endangered Species Act.

Black-and-white Warbler   *Mniotilta varia*

DATE   ☐ *seen*   ☐ *heard*

LOCATION

HABITAT

REMARKS

American Redstart   *Setophaga ruticilla*

DATE   ☐ *seen*   ☐ *heard*

LOCATION

HABITAT

REMARKS

Prothonotary Warbler (PLATE III)

Prothonotary Warbler   *Protonotaria citrea*

DATE   ☐ *seen*   ☐ *heard*

LOCATION

HABITAT

REMARKS

Worm-eating Warbler   *Helmitheros vermivorus*

DATE   ☐ *seen*   ☐ *heard*

LOCATION

HABITAT

REMARKS

Swainson's Warbler   *Limnothlypis swainsonii*

DATE   ☐ *seen*   ☐ *heard*

LOCATION

HABITAT

REMARKS

Ovenbird   *Seiurus aurocapillus*

DATE   ☐ *seen*   ☐ *heard*

LOCATION

HABITAT

REMARKS

The original plate for the Prothonotary Warbler was one of the ten engraved by William Lizars of Edinburgh. When Havell later needed the plate, he unfairly removed Lizar's name from the credit line – much to the latter's chagrin.

Northern Waterthrush   *Seiurus noveboracensis*

DATE   ☐ *seen*   ☐ *heard*

LOCATION

HABITAT

REMARKS

Louisiana Waterthrush   *Seiurus motacilla*

DATE   ☐ *seen*   ☐ *heard*

LOCATION

HABITAT

REMARKS

"Much as the song of the Nightingale is admired," Audubon wrote, "I am inclined to think it no finer than that of the Louisiana Water-Thrush, whose notes are as powerful and mellow and at times as varied."

Kentucky Warbler   *Oporornis formosus*

DATE   ☐ *seen*   ☐ *heard*

LOCATION

HABITAT

REMARKS

Connecticut Warbler   *Oporornis agilis*

DATE   ☐ *seen*   ☐ *heard*

LOCATION

HABITAT

REMARKS

Mourning Warbler *Oporornis philadelphia*

DATE ☐ *seen* ☐ *heard*

LOCATION

HABITAT

REMARKS

MacGillivray's Warbler *Oporornis tolmiei*

DATE ☐ *seen* ☐ *heard*

LOCATION

HABITAT

REMARKS

Common Yellowthroat *Geothlypis trichas*

DATE ☐ *seen* ☐ *heard*

LOCATION

HABITAT

REMARKS

Hooded Warbler *Wilsonia citrina*

DATE ☐ *seen* ☐ *heard*

LOCATION

HABITAT

REMARKS

Common Yellowthroat (Maryland Yellow-throat, PLATE XXIII)

Yellow-breasted Chat (PLATE CXXXVII)

Wilson's Warbler *Wilsonia pusilla*

DATE   ☐ *seen*   ☐ *heard*

LOCATION

HABITAT

REMARKS

Canada Warbler *Wilsonia canadensis*

DATE   ☐ *seen*   ☐ *heard*

LOCATION

HABITAT

REMARKS

Red-faced Warbler *Cardellina rubrifrons*

DATE   ☐ *seen*   ☐ *heard*

LOCATION

HABITAT

REMARKS

Painted Redstart *Myioborus pictus*

DATE   ☐ *seen*   ☐ *heard*

LOCATION

HABITAT

REMARKS

Rufous-capped Warbler   *Basileuterus rufifrons*

DATE   ☐ *seen*   ☐ *heard*

LOCATION

HABITAT

REMARKS

Yellow-breasted Chat   *Icteria virens*

DATE   ☐ *seen*   ☐ *heard*

LOCATION

HABITAT

REMARKS

Olive Warbler   *Peucedramus taeniatus*

DATE   ☐ *seen*   ☐ *heard*

LOCATION

HABITAT

REMARKS

BANANAQUITS   *Emberizidae, subfamily Coerebinae*

Bananaquit   *Coereba flaveola*

DATE   ☐ *seen*   ☐ *heard*

LOCATION

HABITAT

REMARKS

Stripe-headed Tanager   *Spindalis zena*

DATE   ☐ *seen*   ☐ *heard*

LOCATION

HABITAT

REMARKS

Hepatic Tanager   *Piranga flava*

DATE   ☐ *seen*   ☐ *heard*

LOCATION

HABITAT

REMARKS

Summer Tanager   *Piranga rubra*

DATE   ☐ *seen*   ☐ *heard*

LOCATION

HABITAT

REMARKS

Scarlet Tanager   *Piranga olivacea*

DATE   ☐ *seen*   ☐ *heard*

LOCATION

HABITAT

REMARKS

"Tanager" is one of the few bird names to be derived from a Native American language. The word comes from the name of a related bird in Tupi, the language of a New World people that once thrived along the Amazon in what is now Brazil. There are 240 species of tanagers in the world.

Scarlet Tanager & Western Tanager
(Scarlet Tanager & Louisiana Tanager, PLATE CCCLIV)

Western Tanager   *Piranga ludoviciana*

DATE   ☐ *seen*   ☐ *heard*

LOCATION

HABITAT

REMARKS

CARDINALS   *Emberizidae, subfamily Cardinalinae*

Northern Cardinal   *Cardinalis cardinalis*

DATE   ☐ *seen*   ☐ *heard*

LOCATION

HABITAT

REMARKS

Pyrrhuloxia   *Cardinalis sinuatus*

DATE   ☐ *seen*   ☐ *heard*

LOCATION

HABITAT

REMARKS

Rose-breasted Grosbeak   *Pheucticus ludovicianus*

DATE   ☐ *seen*   ☐ *heard*

LOCATION

HABITAT

REMARKS

Northern Cardinal (Cardinal Grosbeak, PLATE CLIX)

Black-headed Grosbeak   *Pheucticus melanocephalus*

DATE   ☐ *seen*   ☐ *heard*

LOCATION

HABITAT

REMARKS

In Edinburgh Audubon briefly had a pet Blue Grosbeak. "He is extremely tame, goes in and out of his cage, perches on the headdress of my wife or on the heads of other members of the family . . . . After bathing he invariably goes to the open fire, and perches on the fender to dry himself."

Blue Grosbeak   *Guiraca caerulea*

DATE   ☐ *seen*   ☐ *heard*

LOCATION

HABITAT

REMARKS

Lazuli Bunting   *Passerina amoena*

DATE   ☐ *seen*   ☐ *heard*

LOCATION

HABITAT

REMARKS

Indigo Bunting   *Passerina cyanea*

DATE   ☐ *seen*   ☐ *heard*

LOCATION

HABITAT

REMARKS

Varied Bunting   *Passerina versicolor*

DATE   ☐ *seen*   ☐ *heard*

LOCATION

HABITAT

REMARKS

Painted Bunting   *Passerina ciris*

DATE   ☐ *seen*   ☐ *heard*

LOCATION

HABITAT

REMARKS

Dickcissel   *Spiza americana*

DATE   ☐ *seen*   ☐ *heard*

LOCATION

HABITAT

REMARKS

NEW WORLD SPARROWS   *Emberizidae, subfamily Emberizinae*

Olive Sparrow   *Arremonops rufivirgatus*

DATE   ☐ *seen*   ☐ *heard*

LOCATION

HABITAT

REMARKS

Green-tailed Towhee	*Pipilo chlorurus*
DATE	☐ *seen* ☐ *heard*
LOCATION	
HABITAT	
REMARKS	

Rufous-sided Towhee	*Pipilo erythrophthalmus*
DATE	☐ *seen* ☐ *heard*
LOCATION	
HABITAT	
REMARKS	

‡THREATENED The California Towhee and the Canyon Towhee are two species recently created out what was formerly the Brown Towhee. One subspecies of California Towhee is threatened by recreational and commercial overuse of southern California's fragile desert.

California Towhee ‡	*Pipilo crissalis*
DATE	☐ *seen* ☐ *heard*
LOCATION	
HABITAT	
REMARKS	

Canyon Towhee	*Pipilo fuscus*
DATE	☐ *seen* ☐ *heard*
LOCATION	
HABITAT	
REMARKS	

Abert's Towhee — *Pipilo aberti*

DATE ☐ *seen* ☐ *heard*

LOCATION

HABITAT

REMARKS

White-collared Seedeater — *Sporophila torqueola*

DATE ☐ *seen* ☐ *heard*

LOCATION

HABITAT

REMARKS

Bachman's Sparrow — *Aimophila aestivalis*

DATE ☐ *seen* ☐ *heard*

LOCATION

HABITAT

REMARKS

The Bachman's Sparrow, named after Audubon's close friend, John Bachman, is a candidate for review under the Endangered Species Act. It may one day be declared threatened or endangered.

Botteri's Sparrow — *Aimophila botterii*

DATE ☐ *seen* ☐ *heard*

LOCATION

HABITAT

REMARKS

Cassin's Sparrow   *Aimophila cassinii*

DATE   ☐ *seen*   ☐ *heard*

LOCATION

HABITAT

REMARKS

Rufous-winged Sparrow   *Aimophila carpalis*

DATE   ☐ *seen*   ☐ *heard*

LOCATION

HABITAT

REMARKS

Rufous-crowned Sparrow   *Aimophila ruficeps*

DATE   ☐ *seen*   ☐ *heard*

LOCATION

HABITAT

REMARKS

American Tree Sparrow   *Spizella arborea*

DATE   ☐ *seen*   ☐ *heard*

LOCATION

HABITAT

REMARKS

Chipping Sparrow *Spizella passerina*

DATE ☐ *seen* ☐ *heard*

LOCATION

HABITAT

REMARKS

Clay-colored Sparrow *Spizella pallida*

DATE ☐ *seen* ☐ *heard*

LOCATION

HABITAT

REMARKS

Brewer's Sparrow *Spizella breweri*

DATE ☐ *seen* ☐ *heard*

LOCATION

HABITAT

REMARKS

Field Sparrow *Spizella pusilla*

DATE ☐ *seen* ☐ *heard*

LOCATION

HABITAT

REMARKS

Black-chinned Sparrow　*Spizella atrogularis*

DATE ☐ *seen* ☐ *heard*

LOCATION

HABITAT

REMARKS

Vesper Sparrow　*Pooecetes gramineus*

DATE ☐ *seen* ☐ *heard*

LOCATION

HABITAT

REMARKS

Lark Sparrow　*Chondestes grammacus*

DATE ☐ *seen* ☐ *heard*

LOCATION

HABITAT

REMARKS

Black-throated Sparrow　*Amphispiza bilineata*

DATE ☐ *seen* ☐ *heard*

LOCATION

HABITAT

REMARKS

Sage Sparrow‡   *Amphispiza belli*

DATE   ☐ *seen*   ☐ *heard*

LOCATION

HABITAT

REMARKS

‡THREATENED   Although one California subspecies of Sage Sparrow, found on San Clemente Island, is officially threatened, at least one other, the Bell's Sage Sparrow, is thought to be declining as well.

Five-striped Sparrow   *Amphispiza quinquestriata*

DATE   ☐ *seen*   ☐ *heard*

LOCATION

HABITAT

REMARKS

Lark Bunting   *Calamospiza melanocorys*

DATE   ☐ *seen*   ☐ *heard*

LOCATION

HABITAT

REMARKS

Savannah Sparrow   *Passerculus sandwichensis*

DATE   ☐ *seen*   ☐ *heard*

LOCATION

HABITAT

REMARKS

Both the Baird's Sparrow and the Henslow's Sparrow are declining. They are both candidates for review under the Endangered Species Act.

Baird's Sparrow   *Ammodramus bairdii*

DATE   ☐ *seen*   ☐ *heard*

LOCATION

HABITAT

REMARKS

‡ENDANGERED Although widespread over much of north America, the Grasshopper Sparrow has not fared well everywhere. The Florida subspecies was declared endangered in 1986.

Grasshopper Sparrow ‡   *Ammodramus savannarum*

DATE   ☐ *seen*   ☐ *heard*

LOCATION

HABITAT

REMARKS

Henslow's Sparrow   *Ammodramus henslowii*

DATE   ☐ *seen*   ☐ *heard*

LOCATION

HABITAT

REMARKS

Le Conte's Sparrow   *Ammodramus leconteii*

DATE   ☐ *seen*   ☐ *heard*

LOCATION

HABITAT

REMARKS

Sharp-tailed Sparrow	*Ammodramus caudacutus*
DATE	☐ *seen* ☐ *heard*
LOCATION	
HABITAT	
REMARKS	

Seaside Sparrow ‡	*Ammodramus maritimus*
DATE	☐ *seen* ☐ *heard*
LOCATION	
HABITAT	
REMARKS	

‡ENDANGERED Development in and around coastal salt-marshes has meant disaster for many Seaside Sparrow subspecies. Removed from the Endangered List in 1990, Florida's Dusky Seaside Sparrow became the first vertebrate to go extinct since the Endangered Species Act was passed in 1973. The Cape Sable subspecies remains endangered, and at least two other Florida subspecies are in trouble.

Fox Sparrow	*Passerella iliaca*
DATE	☐ *seen* ☐ *heard*
LOCATION	
HABITAT	
REMARKS	

Song Sparrow	*Melospiza melodia*
DATE	☐ *seen* ☐ *heard*
LOCATION	
HABITAT	
REMARKS	

Lincoln's Sparrow   *Melospiza lincolnii*

DATE   □ *seen*   □ *heard*

LOCATION

HABITAT

REMARKS

Swamp Sparrow   *Melospiza georgiana*

DATE   □ *seen*   □ *heard*

LOCATION

HABITAT

REMARKS

White-throated Sparrow   *Zonotrichia albicollis*

DATE   □ *seen*   □ *heard*

LOCATION

HABITAT

REMARKS

Golden-crowned Sparrow   *Zonotrichia atricapilla*

DATE   □ *seen*   □ *heard*

LOCATION

HABITAT

REMARKS

White-crowned Sparrow   *Zonotrichia leucophrys*

DATE   ☐ *seen*   ☐ *heard*

LOCATION

HABITAT

REMARKS

After hearing the White-crowned Sparrow sing one day in lonely Labrador, Audubon wrote: " . . how cheering is it to hear the mellow notes of a bird, that seems as if it had been sent expressly for the purpose of relieving your mind from the heavy melancholy that bears it down!"

Harris' Sparrow   *Zonotrichia querula*

DATE   ☐ *seen*   ☐ *heard*

LOCATION

HABITAT

REMARKS

Dark-eyed Junco   *Junco hyemalis*

DATE   ☐ *seen*   ☐ *heard*

LOCATION

HABITAT

REMARKS

Yellow-eyed Junco   *Junco phaeonotus*

DATE   ☐ *seen*   ☐ *heard*

LOCATION

HABITAT

REMARKS

Swamp Sparrow (PLATE LXIV)

McCown's Longspur   *Calcarius mccownii*

DATE   ☐ *seen*   ☐ *heard*

LOCATION

HABITAT

REMARKS

Lapland Longspur   *Calcarius lapponicus*

DATE   ☐ *seen*   ☐ *heard*

LOCATION

HABITAT

REMARKS

Smith's Longspur   *Calcarius pictus*

DATE   ☐ *seen*   ☐ *heard*

LOCATION

HABITAT

REMARKS

REMARKS

Chestnut-collared Longspur   *Calcarius ornatus*

DATE   ☐ *seen*   ☐ *heard*

LOCATION

HABITAT

REMARKS

Rustic Bunting   *Emberiza rustica*

DATE   ☐ *seen*   ☐ *heard*

LOCATION

HABITAT

REMARKS

Snow Bunting   *Plectrophenax nivalis*

DATE   ☐ *seen*   ☐ *heard*

LOCATION

HABITAT

REMARKS

McKay's Bunting   *Plectrophenax hyperboreus*

DATE   ☐ *seen*   ☐ *heard*

LOCATION

HABITAT

REMARKS

Bobolink   *Dolichonyx oryzivorus*

DATE   ☐ *seen*   ☐ *heard*

LOCATION

HABITAT

REMARKS

Red-winged Blackbird   *Agelaius phoeniceus*

DATE   ☐ *seen*   ☐ *heard*

LOCATION

HABITAT

REMARKS

Tricolored Blackbird   *Agelaius tricolor*

DATE   ☐ *seen*   ☐ *heard*

LOCATION

HABITAT

REMARKS

The Tricolored Blackbird is declining and is a candidate for status review under the Endangered Species Act.

Eastern Meadowlark   *Sturnella magna*

DATE   ☐ *seen*   ☐ *heard*

LOCATION

HABITAT

REMARKS

Western Meadowlark   *Sturnella neglecta*

DATE   ☐ *seen*   ☐ *heard*

LOCATION

HABITAT

REMARKS

Yellow-headed Blackbird   *Xanthocephalus xanthocephalus*

DATE   ☐ *seen*   ☐ *heard*

LOCATION

HABITAT

REMARKS

Rusty Blackbird   *Euphagus carolinus*

DATE   ☐ *seen*   ☐ *heard*

LOCATION

HABITAT

REMARKS

Brewer's Blackbird   *Euphagus cyanocephalus*

DATE   ☐ *seen*   ☐ *heard*

LOCATION

HABITAT

REMARKS

Great-tailed Grackle   *Quiscalus mexicanus*

DATE   ☐ *seen*   ☐ *heard*

LOCATION

HABITAT

REMARKS

Orchard Oriole (PLATE XLII)

Boat-tailed Grackle   *Quiscalus major*

DATE   ☐ *seen*   ☐ *heard*

LOCATION

HABITAT

REMARKS

Common Grackle   *Quiscalus quiscula*

DATE   ☐ *seen*   ☐ *heard*

LOCATION

HABITAT

REMARKS

Bronzed Cowbird   *Molothrus aeneus*

DATE   ☐ *seen*   ☐ *heard*

LOCATION

HABITAT

REMARKS

Brown-headed Cowbird   *Molothrus ater*

DATE   ☐ *seen*   ☐ *heard*

LOCATION

HABITAT

REMARKS

Orchard Oriole   *Icterus spurius*

DATE   ☐ *seen*   ☐ *heard*

LOCATION

HABITAT

REMARKS

"The sociability of the Orchard Oriole is quite remarkable," Audubon observed after counting nine occupied nests within a few acres. "The nest in *The Birds of America*, drawn in Louisiana, was entirely of grass and shows the usual form and construction."

Hooded Oriole   *Icterus cucullatus*

DATE   ☐ *seen*   ☐ *heard*

LOCATION

HABITAT

REMARKS

Streak-backed Oriole   *Icterus pustulatus*

DATE   ☐ *seen*   ☐ *heard*

LOCATION

HABITAT

REMARKS

Spot-breasted Oriole   *Icterus pectoralis*

DATE   ☐ *seen*   ☐ *heard*

LOCATION

HABITAT

REMARKS

Altamira Oriole   *Icterus gularis*

DATE   ☐ *seen*   ☐ *heard*

LOCATION

HABITAT

REMARKS

Sadly, the status of the uncommon Audubon's Oriole is unknown. It is a candidate for review under the Endangered Species Act, and may one day be listed as threatened or endangered.

Audubon's Oriole   *Icterus graduacauda*

DATE   ☐ *seen*   ☐ *heard*

LOCATION

HABITAT

REMARKS

Northern Oriole   *Icterus galbula*

DATE   ☐ *seen*   ☐ *heard*

LOCATION

HABITAT

REMARKS

Scott's Oriole   *Icterus parisorum*

DATE   ☐ *seen*   ☐ *heard*

LOCATION

HABITAT

REMARKS

Brambling   *Fringilla montifringilla*

DATE   ☐ *seen*   ☐ *heard*

LOCATION

HABITAT

REMARKS

Rosy Finch   *Leucosticte arctoa*

DATE   ☐ *seen*   ☐ *heard*

LOCATION

HABITAT

REMARKS

Pine Grosbeak   *Pinicola enucleator*

DATE   ☐ *seen*   ☐ *heard*

LOCATION

HABITAT

REMARKS

In Newfoundland, Audubon found Pine Grosbeaks with sores on their legs, "due, I believe, to the resin on the fir trees where they feed." The sores, he said, "sometimes cause the back of the lower leg joint to be double the usual size."

Purple Finch   *Carpodacus purpureus*

DATE   ☐ *seen*   ☐ *heard*

LOCATION

HABITAT

REMARKS

Cassin's Finch   *Carpodacus cassinii*

DATE   ☐ *seen*   ☐ *heard*

LOCATION

HABITAT

REMARKS

House Finch   *Carpodacus mexicanus*

DATE   ☐ *seen*   ☐ *heard*

LOCATION

HABITAT

REMARKS

Red Crossbill   *Loxia curvirostra*

DATE   ☐ *seen*   ☐ *heard*

LOCATION

HABITAT

REMARKS

White-winged Crossbill   *Loxia leucoptera*

DATE   ☐ *seen*   ☐ *heard*

LOCATION

HABITAT

REMARKS

Common Redpoll — *Carduelis flammea*

DATE   ☐ *seen*   ☐ *heard*

LOCATION

HABITAT

REMARKS

Hoary Redpoll — *Carduelis hornemanni*

DATE   ☐ *seen*   ☐ *heard*

LOCATION

HABITAT

REMARKS

Pine Siskin — *Carduelis pinus*

DATE   ☐ *seen*   ☐ *heard*

LOCATION

HABITAT

REMARKS

Lesser Goldfinch — *Carduelis psaltria*

DATE   ☐ *seen*   ☐ *heard*

LOCATION

HABITAT

REMARKS

FINCHES   *Fringillidae*

Lawrence's Goldfinch   *Carduelis lawrencei*

DATE   ☐ *seen*   ☐ *heard*

LOCATION

HABITAT

REMARKS

American Goldfinch   *Carduelis tristis*

DATE   ☐ *seen*   ☐ *heard*

LOCATION

HABITAT

REMARKS

Evening Grosbeak   *Coccothraustes vespertinus*

DATE   ☐ *seen*   ☐ *heard*

LOCATION

HABITAT

REMARKS

OLD WORLD SPARROWS   *Passeridae*

House Sparrow   *Passer domesticus*

DATE   ☐ *seen*   ☐ *heard*

LOCATION

HABITAT

REMARKS

Eurasian Tree Sparrow   *Passer montanus*

DATE   ☐ *seen*   ☐ *heard*

LOCATION

HABITAT

REMARKS

NOTES

CREDITS

The reproductions in this book are from *The Birds of America*, 1827-1838, by John James Audubon (American, 1785-1851), in the collection of the Print Department of the Museum of Fine Arts, Boston. They appear here in Audubon's original plate order.

Prothonotary Warbler (PLATE III)
Etching and aquatint with hand-coloring in watercolor by Robert Havell, Jr. (British, 1785-1878)
20^1/$_2$ x 12^1/$_2$ inches
Gift of William Hooper
21.11772.3

Bewick's Long-tailed Wren (PLATE XVIII)
Etching and aquatint with hand-coloring in watercolor by Robert Havell, Jr. (British, 1785-1878)
19^5/$_8$ x 12^1/$_8$ inches
Gift of William Hooper
21.11772.18

Yellow-breasted Warbler/Maryland Yellow Throat (PLATE XXIII)
Etching and aquatint with hand-coloring in watercolor by Robert Havell, Jr. (British, 1785-1878)
19^3/$_8$ x 12^1/$_8$ inches
Gift of William Hooper
21.11772.23

Solitary Flycatcher or Vireo (Plate XXVIII)
Etching and aquatint with hand-coloring in watercolor by Robert Havell, Jr. (British, 1785-1878)
19^1/$_2$ x 12^1/$_4$ inches
Gift of William Hooper
21.11772.28

Crested Titmouse (PLATE XXXIX)
Etching and aquatint with hand-coloring in watercolor by Robert Havell, Jr. (British, 1785-1878)
19^1/$_2$ x 12^1/$_4$ inches
Gift of William Hooper
21.11772.39

Orchard Oriole (PLATE XLII)
Etching and aquatint with hand-coloring in watercolor by Robert Havell, Jr. (British, 1785-1878)
26 x 20^7/$_8$ inches
Gift of William Hooper
21.11772.42

Cedar Bird (PLATE XLIII)
Etching and aquatint with hand-coloring in watercolor by Robert Havell, Jr. (British, 1785-1878)
19^5/$_8$ x 12^1/$_4$ inches
Gift of William Hooper
21.11772.43

Chestnut-sided Warbler (PLATE LIX)
Etching and aquatint with hand-coloring in watercolor by Robert Havell, Jr. (British, 1785-1878)
19^1/$_2$ x 12^1/$_4$ inches
Gift of William Hooper
21.11772.59

Red Shouldered Hawk (PLATE LVI)
Etching and aquatint with hand-coloring in watercolor by Robert Havell, Jr. (British, 1785-1878)
38^1/$_8$ x 25^1/$_2$ inches
Gift of William Hooper
21.11772.61

Passenger Pigeon (PLATE LXII)
Etching and aquatint with hand-coloring in watercolor by Robert Havell, Jr. (British, 1785-1878)
26 x 20^7/$_8$ inches
Gift of William Hooper
21.11772.62

Swamp Sparrow (PLATE LXIV)
Etching and aquatint with hand-coloring in watercolor by Robert Havell, Jr. (British, 1785-1878)
19^3/$_8$ x 12^1/$_4$ inches
Gift of William Hooper
21.11772.64

Ivory-billed Woodpecker (PLATE LXVI)
Etching and aquatint with hand-coloring in watercolor by Robert Havell, Jr. (British, 1785-1878)
38^1/$_4$ x 25^5/$_8$ inches
Gift of William Hooper
21.11772.66

Brown Pelican (PLATE CCLI)
Etching and aquatint with hand-coloring in watercolor by
Robert Havell, Jr. (British, 1785-1878)
38^1/$_8$ x 25^1/$_2$ inches
Gift of William Hooper
21.11772.251

Hooping Crane (PLATE CCLXI)
Etching and aquatint with hand-coloring in watercolor by
Robert Havell, Jr. (British, 1785-1878)
38^1/$_8$ x 25^1/$_2$ inches
Gift of William Hooper
21.11772.261

Pigmy Curlew (PLATE CCLXIII)
Etching and aquatint with hand-coloring in watercolor by
Robert Havell, Jr. (British, 1785-1878)
12^1/$_8$ x 19^1/$_4$ inches
Gift of William Hooper
21.11772.263

Fork-tailed Gull (PLATE CCLXXXV)
Etching and aquatint with hand-coloring in watercolor by
Robert Havell, Jr. (British, 1785-1878)
12^1/$_4$ x 19^1/$_4$ inches
Gift of William Hooper
21.11772.285

Canvas-backed Duck (PLATE CCCI)
Etching and aquatint with hand-coloring in watercolor by
Robert Havell, Jr. (British, 1785-1878)
25^1/$_2$ x 38^1/$_8$ inches
Gift of William Hooper
21.11772.301

Blue Heron (PLATE CCCVII)
Etching and aquatint with hand-coloring in watercolor by
Robert Havell, Jr. (British, 1785-1878)
21^1/$_4$ x 30^1/$_2$ inches
Gift of William Hooper
21.11772.307

Long-tailed Duck (PLATE CCCXII)
Etching and aquatint with hand-coloring in watercolor by
Robert Havell, Jr. (British, 1785-1878)
21^1/$_4$ x 30^1/$_4$ inches
Gift of William Hooper
21.11772.312

Blue-Winged Teal (PLATE CCCXIII)
Etching and aquatint with hand-coloring in watercolor by
Robert Havell, Jr. (British, 1785-1878)
14^3/$_4$ x 20^1/$_2$ inches
Gift of William Hooper
21.11772.313

Black-headed Gull (PLATE CCCXIV)
Etching and aquatint with hand-coloring in watercolor by
Robert Havell, Jr. (British, 1785-1878)
14^3/$_4$ x 20^1/$_2$ inches
Gift of William Hooper
21.11772.314

American Avocet (PLATE CCCXVIII)
Etching and aquatint with hand-coloring in watercolor by
Robert Havell, Jr. (British, 1785-1878)
14^5/$_8$ x 20^3/$_8$ inches
Gift of William Hooper
21.11772.318

Buffel-headed Duck (PLATE CCCXXV)
Etching and aquatint with hand-coloring in watercolor by
Robert Havell, Jr. (British, 1785-1878)
14^7/$_8$ x 20^1/$_2$ inches
Gift of William Hooper
21.11772.325

Goosander (PLATE CCCXXXI)
Etching and aquatint with hand-coloring in watercolor by
Robert Havell, Jr. (British, 1785-1878)
25^5/$_8$ x 38^1/$_4$ inches
Gift of William Hooper
21.11772.331

American Bittern (PLATE CCCXXXVII)
Etching and aquatint with hand-coloring in watercolor by
Robert Havell, Jr. (British, 1785-1878)
22^7/$_8$ x 28^1/$_8$ inches
Gift of William Hooper
21.11772.337

American Widgeon (PLATE CCCXLV)
Etching and aquatint with hand-coloring in watercolor by
Robert Havell, Jr. (British, 1785-1878)
15 x 20 inches
Gift of William Hooper
21.11772.345

Great Cinereous Owl (PLATE CCCLI)
Etching and aquatint with hand-coloring in watercolor by
Robert Havell, Jr. (British, 1785-1878)
38^1/$_4$ x 25^5/$_8$ inches
Gift of William Hooper
21.11772.351

Scarlet Tanager & Louisiana Tanager (PLATE CCCLIV)
Etching and aquatint with hand-coloring in watercolor by
Robert Havell, Jr. (British, 1785-1878)
19^7/$_8$ x 12^3/$_8$ inches
Gift of William Hooper
21.11772.354

Fish Hawk (PLATE LXXXI)
Etching and aquatint with hand-coloring in watercolor by
Robert Havell, Jr. (British, 1785-1878)
38¼ x 25⅝ inches
Gift of William Hooper
21.11772.81

Yellow-throated Warbler (PLATE LXXXV)
Etching and aquatint with hand-coloring in watercolor by
Robert Havell, Jr. (British, 1785-1878)
19⅜ x 12¼ inches
Gift of William Hooper
21.11772.85

Blue-bird (PLATE CXIII)
Etching and aquatint with hand-coloring in watercolor by
Robert Havell, Jr. (British, 1785-1878)
19¼ x 12⅜ inches
Gift of William Hooper
21.11772.113

Snowy Owl (PLATE CXXI)
Etching and aquatint with hand-coloring in watercolor by
Robert Havell, Jr. (British, 1785-1878)
38¼ x 25⅝ inches
Gift of William Hooper
21.11772.121

Yellow-breasted Chat (PLATE CXXXVII)
Etching and aquatint with hand-coloring in watercolor by
Robert Havell, Jr. (British, 1785-1878)
25¾ x 20⅝ inches
Gift of William Hooper
21.11772.137

Yellow Red-poll Warbler (PLATE CXLV)
Etching and aquatint with hand-coloring in watercolor by
Robert Havell, Jr. (British, 1785-1878)
19½ x 12⅜ inches
Gift of William Hooper
21.11772.145

Black-throated Blue Warbler (PLATE CLV)
Etching and aquatint with hand-coloring in watercolor by
Robert Havell, Jr. (British, 1785-1878)
19⅝ x 12⅜ inches
Gift of William Hooper
21.11772.155

Cardinal Grosbeak (PLATE CLIX)
Etching and aquatint with hand-coloring in watercolor by
Robert Havell, Jr. (British, 1785-1878)
19⅜ x 12¼ inches
Gift of William Hooper
21.11772.159

Barn Swallow (PLATE CLXXIII)
Etching and aquatint with hand-coloring in watercolor by
Robert Havell, Jr. (British, 1785-1878)
19½ x 12¼ inches
Gift of William Hooper
21.11772.173

Willow Grous or Large Ptarmigan (PLATE CXCI)
Etching and aquatint with hand-coloring in watercolor by
Robert Havell, Jr. (British, 1785-1878)
25⅝ x 38¼ inches
Gift of William Hooper
21.11772.191

Great Blue Heron (PLATE CCXI)
Etching and aquatint with hand-coloring in watercolor by
Robert Havell, Jr. (British, 1785-1878)
38⅛ x 25½ inches
Gift of William Hooper
21.11772.211

Puffin (PLATE CCXIII)
Etching and aquatint with hand-coloring in watercolor by
Robert Havell, Jr. (British, 1785-1878)
12¼ x 19½ inches
Gift of William Hooper
21.11772.213

Louisiana Heron (PLATE CCXVII)
Etching and aquatint with hand-coloring in watercolor by
Robert Havell, Jr. (British, 1785-1878)
20¾ x 25⅞ inches
Gift of William Hooper
21.11772.217

Green-Winged Teal (PLATE CCXXVIII)
Etching and aquatint with hand-coloring in watercolor by
Robert Havell, Jr. (British, 1785-1878)
12¼ x 19⅜ inches
Gift of William Hooper
21.11772.228

Night Heron or Qua Bird (PLATE CCXXXVI)
Etching and aquatint with hand-coloring in watercolor by
Robert Havell, Jr. (British, 1785-1878)
25½ x 38⅛ inches
Gift of William Hooper
21.11772.236

Snowy Heron or White Egret (PLATE CCXLII)
Etching and aquatint with hand-coloring in watercolor by
Robert Havell, Jr. (British, 1785-1878)
25¾ x 20½ inches
Gift of William Hooper
21.11772.242

Rufous Hummingbird (Ruff-necked Humming-bird)
(PLATE CCCLXXIX)
Etching and aquatint with hand-coloring in watercolor by
Robert Havell, Jr. (British, 1785-1878)
$19^5/_8$ x $12^3/_8$ inches
Gift of William Hooper
21.11772.379

Glossy Ibis (PLATE CCCLXXXVII)
Etching and aquatint with hand-coloring in watercolor by
Robert Havell, Jr. (British, 1785-1878)
$21^7/_8$ x $26^1/_8$ inches
Gift of William Hooper
21.11772.387

Artic Blue-bird, Townsend's Warbler & Western Blue-bird
(PLATE CCCXCIII)
Etching and aquatint with hand-coloring in watercolor by
Robert Havell, Jr. (British, 1785-1878)
$19^1/_2$ x $12^3/_8$ inches
Gift of William Hooper
21.11772.393

Golden-eye Duck (PLATE CCCCIII)
Etching and aquatint with hand-coloring in watercolor by
Robert Havell, Jr. (British, 1785-1878)
$12^1/_4$ x $19^1/_2$ inches
Gift of William Hooper
21.11772.403

Semipalmated Sandpiper (PLATE CCCCV)
Etching and aquatint with hand-coloring in watercolor by
Robert Havell, Jr. (British, 1785-1878)
$12^3/_8$ x $19^1/_2$ inches
Gift of William Hooper
21.11772.405

Common American Swan (PLATE CCCCXI)
Etching and aquatint with hand-coloring in watercolor by
Robert Havell, Jr. (British, 1785-1878)
$25^5/_8$ x $38^1/_4$ inches
Gift of William Hooper
21.11772.411

Brown Creeper & California Nuthatch (LATE CCCCXV)
Etching and aquatint with hand-coloring in watercolor by
Robert Havell, Jr. (British, 1785-1878)
$19^1/_2$ x $12^1/_2$ inches
Gift of William Hooper
21.11772.415

Anna's Hummingbird (Columbian Hummingbird)
(PLATE CCCCXXV)
Etching and aquatint with hand-coloring in watercolor by
Robert Havell, Jr. (British, 1785-1878)
$19^1/_2$ x $12^1/_4$ inches
Gift of William Hooper
21.11772.425

American Flamingo (PLATE CCCCXXXI)
Etching and aquatint with hand-coloring in watercolor by
Robert Havell, Jr. (British, 1785-1878)
$38^1/_4$ x $25^5/_8$ inches
Gift of William Hooper
21.11772.431

INDEX